W9-BQZ-001

HYMNS IN THE LIVES OF MEN

HYMNS IN THE LIVES OF MEN

by

Robert Guy McCutchan

THE FIRST ANNUAL
SOUTHWESTERN UNIVERSITY LECTURES
Georgetown, Texas, 1943

ABINGDON-COKESBURY PRESS
New York • *Nashville*

HYMNS IN THE LIVES OF MEN

COPYRIGHT, MCMXLV
By WHITMORE & STONE

K

PRINTED IN THE UNITED STATES OF AMERICA

PREFACE

IN THIS BOOK AN ATTEMPT IS MADE TO CLARIFY THE MEANings attached to the word "worship"; to show why hymns have always held such a prominent place and have always been such an important element in worship; to question the soundness of the position of those who would have us believe the early Hebrew poets received their poetic and spiritual inspiration from pagan sources; to call attention to the fact that, from the earliest days of Christianity, psalms, chants, canticles, hymns, and other types of sacred song have, for good, influenced men in all walks of life. Whether the days have been days of war or peace, pestilence or well-being, poverty or plenty, sickness or health, solace has been found in hymns; they have aided in alleviating misery, in mitigating or dispelling distress of mind or spirit; they have been a means of giving vocal expression to joy and happiness. Poets, seldom satisfied with the *status quo,* have always been found among dissenters; so, whenever and wherever heresy has raised its ugly head and schism has threatened or developed, the hymn writer has been right there to take his part in the controversy and to make his contribution to the cause of one side or of both.

The highway along which the Church has trod has been followed; and where we discover its life and work has been most intense, there we find our richest hymnody. The most conclusive evidence of the validity and vitality of our Christian faith is shown in those hymns which have been written when that faith was being sorely tried, most seriously threatened, and when it seemed about to be totally eclipsed. Both the life and the corruption of the Church throughout the darkness of the Middle Ages may be traced through its hymnic literature. It has been said that "the Divine Spirit has always employed the ministry of that poetry which was the poetry of the age." Results of the ministry of hymns, in evidence during the Reformation on the continent of Europe and in England, as well as in the "great awakenings" in this country, have accompanied Christians around the world.

As hymns have a deeper meaning and a more living interest if thought of in connection with, and in their relation to, the period and situation which produced them, their chronological sequence has been followed in so far as has been feasible.

The most effective bond between Christians today is found in the hymns which are common to the peoples of all faiths and creeds, for time has proven them true to the general experience of Christians. Millions of people every week sing hymns in their services of public worship; in their private devotions hymns are no less helpful. It is safe to say we have no medium of expression which is more helpful by way of nourishment of our spiritual lives and religious culture.

Some criticism may be raised because of the sympathetic treatment accorded the gospel song. The only answer to such criticism as there may be is that literary and musical excellence has not been the sole criterion in the selection of material used for purposes of illustration.

Although most, if not all, of the hymns mentioned or discussed are common to our more recent hymnals, the reference numbers are those of *The Methodist Hymnal* of 1935.

PREFACE

Among the reasons for the selection of this particular book are the author's familiarity with it, the desirability of focusing the reader's attention, and the amazing fact that some two million of these hymnals have been sold and are to be found not only in Methodist churches and homes but in those of other communions. The author suggests that a copy of the music edition of *The Methodist Hymnal* be kept at hand and that the numbered references be sung as they are being read. For hymns are written to be sung, not just read or talked about; and through singing one is enabled to give expression to a type of feeling which he does not experience when merely reading. It should be remembered that "feeling conditions reflection" to an extent not always fully appreciated.

In the minds of the thoughtful there can be no doubt that hymns have been and continue to be a tremendous force for good in the lives of men. Through hymns Christianity has provided its adherents a means of individual expression such as no other religion possesses. The continuity of hymn writing has been so constant that what was said by Christian poets centuries ago is, in some instances, being repeated in almost the same words by certain of them in our own day. This book goes on its way in the hope that it may play some little part in strengthening the devotion of men and women who are earnestly striving to bring about the Kingdom of God on earth in their time.

I wish to express my gratitude to publishers and other owners who have been so generous in allowing me free use of their copyright material. Every effort has been made to give proper acknowledgment for the use of anything which is not the author's own. And I wish, further, to extend my thanks to Luther Freeman, Harland E. Hogue, Mary Elizabeth Blanchard, and others who have read the manuscript in whole or in part and who have made helpful criticisms and suggestions. To Mary Jane Stewart and Bernice Johnson, who assisted in the preparation of the manuscript for the publishers, I am grateful.

ROBERT G. MCCUTCHAN

HYMNS IN THE LIVES OF MEN

I.	WHAT IS WORSHIP?	11
II.	WHAT IS A HYMN?	21
III.	PAGAN SOURCES?	39
IV.	THE PSALMS	61
V.	CHANTS AND CANTICLES	72
VI.	EARLY GREEK AND LATIN HYMNS	88
VII.	LATER LATIN HYMNS AND SEQUENCES	104
VIII.	CHORALES AND METRICAL PSALMS	120
IX.	ENGLAND'S DEVELOPMENT OF THE HYMN	138
X.	OUR AMERICAN HERITAGE AND CONTRIBUTION	155
XI.	THE ECUMENICAL TREND IN HYMNODY	174
	REFERENCES	191
	INDEX OF HYMNS, STANZAS, SONGS	195
	GENERAL INDEX	199

I

WHAT IS WORSHIP?

ABOUT A.D. 60 THERE WAS BORN IN GREECE A BOY CHILD who became the slave of Epaphroditus, a Roman. Despite the fact that he was small, lame, and weakly, he endured severe treatment with heroic equanimity, devoted all possible time to study, seized every opportunity to improve his mind, and eventually gained his freedom. Not knowing his original name and finding it desirable as a free man to have one, he adopted one, "Epictetus," meaning "Acquired," and as Epictetus has become known as one of the Stoic philosophers whose ethics teach self-renunciation, endurance, and the limiting of ambition. His philosophy shows a high idealistic type of morality. True education, he taught, lies in recognizing that there is only one thing which is our own, namely, our will, or purpose. Epictetus left no writings; his pupil, Arrian, the historian of Alexander the Great, collected certain of his maxims in the work entitled *Enchiridion*—"Handbook"—and in some eight books of *Discourses,* four of which have been lost.

Among his sayings is one which is worthy of attention: *Since I am a reasonable creature it is my duty to praise God. This is my business; I do it; nor will I ever desert this post as long as it is vouchsafed to me; and I exhort you to join in the same song.*

There are two elements of worship which are very important. The first is an activity of the mind. Very few people, for instance, know what to do during a period of silence in a service. And the second is this: the close relationship between faith and a feeling of worship. Worship is likely to be destroyed by insincerity unless there is a genuine confidence in the value and validity of the presence of the Unseen. It is, to be sure, a feeling, but a feeling that should grow out of a deep, underlying confidence. It was nothing especially noteworthy that John Wesley's heart was "strangely warmed" at Aldersgate Street. What caused it to remain warm through the years? It was his faith.

The old Latin proverb *Semper agens, semper quietus*—"Always active, always tranquil"—is suggestive. It is worth while to think of its implications, for both elements are in worship; both grow out of that deep, underlying confidence in the reality and authenticity of the Unseen.

It is difficult to define the word "worship" clearly and adequately. When Hugh Benson said, "The worship of Almighty God is the highest act in which a human being can participate," he did not define anything; he merely made a statement. An attempt, however, will be made to make more clear the meaning of this word, especially in its corporate sense.

Worship, the noun, is defined in such dictionaries as I have consulted as an act of paying divine honors—such as reverence, homage, adoration, sacrifice, praise, prayer, thanksgiving —to the Supreme Being, or to a god, as a religious exercise. While definitions vary somewhat, "reverence," "homage," and "adoration" are commonly used as defining words.

Reverence is a feeling of respect, admiration, and awe; veneration; esteem heightened by awe, especially when such a feeling is expressed toward deity.

Homage is an act of reverence or respect paid by external

action; it is an obeisance—that is, a movement of the body, a gesture in token of respect. (In feudal law homage meant an acknowledgment, or admission, of fealty to a lord and of tenure under him. It was a public ceremony which bound the vassal to the lord, whose man he thereupon became, and under whom he held the land for which he was to render his service.)

Adoration may be said to be the supreme worship due to God alone.

In true worship, then, there should be a feeling of awe and the showing of respect, by external action, of such character as one would show Almighty God alone. One who wishes to give further consideration to the word and its implications need but remember that it comes from the old Anglo-Saxon noun "worthship." Here further defining will aid us.

"Worth" means something having good qualities; something of value; a thing of honor and dignity. We frequently misuse this word. We go into a store, look at an article, and inquire, "What is this worth?" That is not at all what we want to know; what we should say in order to secure the information we seek is, "How much money am I going to have to pay for this if I get it?" We confuse "worth" and "price": the price is frequently high, the worth low; seldom is it the other way around.

"Ship" is simply a noun-forming suffix, originally used with adjectives. It may denote quality or state, in which case we have such a word as friendship; it may denote art or skill, and a word such as craftsmanship or horsemanship results. Or it may denote something *embodying* state or quality, giving us such words as courtship (act of paying court) or worship (courtesy or reverence paid to merit or worth).

But it may be well to note that the suffix not only *denotes,* that is, points out; it also *connotes* certain things—things in addition to the explicit or recognized signification.

Public worship (and the private devotions of an individual for that matter) should be reverential, inspiring, restful; it should be simple, yet fervid, and filled with spiritual unction —and by "unction" is meant that quality in address, language, or the like which shows or moves one to sober and fervent emotion. James Gibbon Huneker said: "God cannot be worshiped beautifully enough"; the Psalmist said, "Holiness becometh thine house, O Lord, for ever."

Summing up, then, we might say worship embodies something that is good, is of value, is honorable, that has dignity, with inspiring, intelligent, restful reverence, and homage, the last being paid by external action.

Yet, this does not tell all that worship is. Those things the word connotes and which cannot be defined by other words are the things which are most significant.

Can one understand or comprehend worship who has never tried to worship? Can one who is color-blind appreciate a description of a sunset? Can one who is tone-deaf appreciate a symphony?

Sunsets and symphonies may be described in detail; so may worship. Yet, much as we may talk about its various elements, we may never experience it.

Have you ever attended a concert where all the conditions for listening to music were just right? Where the room was acoustically satisfactory? Where the decorations were pleasing to the eye? Where the seats were so comfortable you were not conscious of them? Where the instruments were in perfect tune? Where the numbers played were not so familiar to you as to prejudice you in any way as to their interpretation, yet familiar enough to you so that you might follow the unfolding musical scheme without effort? If so, you have had an experience you can neither define nor describe. This writer has never been able to tell anyone of the feeling which came over him when, years ago in Dresden, he first saw the Sistine Madonna; it would be useless for him to attempt it.

We all have—or have we?—attended religious services where something happened which was not indicated in the matter on the printed order, where holiness pervaded the house, where hearts were "strangely warmed" as was John Wesley's heart at Aldersgate Street. That is what worship should mean for one.

But such occasions do not just happen. Someone has given much thought to the preparation of those elements which comprise any service which will affect people so. It is true that one does not need to come into the dining room by way of the kitchen to enjoy the dinner, that one does not need to be a trained musician in order to be thrilled by music, and that one need not know all of the technique of worship to be benefited by it. Yet if the meal is palatable and nourishing, it must be prepared by an expert; if the music is great music, the composer must have been trained in music. So, if we are to have effective worship, those responsible for our public services of worship should conscientiously study it in order that they may know what they are trying to do and what it is all about. Those who have such responsibility need to be alert to provide that which is beautiful and wholesome, to be ever aware that Christian worship is an inexhaustible source of life and power.

Few of us are mystics in the Quietist or Pietist sense, that is, in the sense that we hold possible a direct or conscious and unmistakable intercourse with God through a species of ecstasy. Yet, in the sense of being conscious that there are some things which are obscure to human knowledge, many of us may be.

> I know not how that Bethlehem's Babe
>   Could in the Godhead be;
> I only know the manger Child
>   Has brought God's life to me.
>
> I know not how that Calvary's cross
>   A world from sin could free;
> I only know its matchless love
>   Has brought God's love to me.
>
> I know not how that Joseph's tomb
>   Could solve death's mystery;
> I only know a living Christ,
>   Our immortality.[1]

Surely we worship when we sing that thoughtfully and sincerely; surely it has in it the elements both of reverence and awe.

And if, as was stated in the Scottish Directory, "one primary design of the public ordinances is to pay social acts of homage to the Most High God," are we not paying such homage when we stand and sing together: "All hail the power of Jesus' name"—"Go, spread your trophies at His feet"—"We at His feet may fall"—"Crown Him Lord of all"? Of course, we may not literally fall at His feet or spread our trophies there; but we may, standing and singing, reaffirm our fidelity and loyalty to our Lord.

Each Wednesday morning during the college year at De-

Pauw University at the regular daily chapel hour there is held what is called A Service of Worship. The length of the period is twenty minutes, and attendance by faculty members and students is purely voluntary, as it is at all of the chapel services at that institution. In the early 1930's, as a result of some conversations with students, it was decided to try the experiment of making one of the daily chapel periods each week a purely devotional service. After much thought and careful planning announcement was made that on a certain Wednesday the chapel service would be held in the Methodist church adjoining the campus and that it would be a service of worship. There were some misgivings in certain quarters as to what would happen; no one knew, of course, just what might happen. But some, a very few it is true, were convinced there were some students in the University who were sincerely desirous of having the privilege, at least, of attending some such service as had been planned. There was no way of telling in advance how many of the twelve or thirteen hundred young people in the student body might want such a thing, but it was felt that if no more than fifty would respond it would be well worth the effort. Imagine the surprise of the sponsors of the service when more than a thousand students came to the first one. The leaders were skeptical; they wondered if the novelty of the innovation had not been the attraction; they were sure it would not happen again.

Apparently its novelty was not the attraction: such weekly services have been held during the succeeding years, and the attendance averages several hundred each Wednesday. What had happened? The sponsors didn't know; they were simply thankful it was so.

What is done? Nothing which may not be done in any college or church or in any place where there may be groups of people. There is a Processional in which all join from the beginning of the first stanza of the hymn, an Organ Meditation which is a short period of silence on the part of the worshipers, a Unison Prayer, a Congregational Hymn, a Unison Scripture Reading (*not* a Responsive Reading), a short, appropriate special musical number by the choir, an Address of not more than six minutes in length, the whole closing with a Choral Prayer, sung by all, which more often than not is a stanza of some familiar hymn such as:

> Saviour, again to Thy dear Name we raise
> With one accord our parting hymn of praise;
> We stand to bless Thee ere our worship cease,
> And still our hearts to wait Thy word of peace.

There are occasional speakers from off the campus, but most frequently they are chosen from among the members of the faculty of the University. There is no duty of the faculty members which is taken more seriously by them; and, apparently, no invitation to speak publicly which may come to them is prized more highly by them. The service is one of worship in its truest sense; it is helpful not only to those in the pews but equally so to those in the pulpit and in the choir loft.

If any one thing has been emphasized during the years it is the element of participation by all in practically the entire service—there are "*social acts* of homage to the Most High God." All have equal opportunity for participation in all parts of the service except the special musical number and the address.

For the first several years, during the period when the custom was becoming fixed, care was taken to avoid even the slightest suggestion of publicizing this quite unusual service. No special announcements were made concerning any of the speakers. A printed Order of Worship has been provided for each service, and it is a very significant thing that few of them are left behind in the pews. Many students are known to have kept all of them during their four years in college, on occasion asking friends to bring them one when, for any reason, they have found it impossible to attend a service; there are members of the faculty who have complete files of them.

Neither students nor faculty members seem to be conscious that they are doing anything unusual in attending and participating in the services; it seems, and is, such a normal thing to do.

Each year at the University, in Course 101, English Composition, required of all Freshmen, at least one assignment given is for a theme on any subject of the student's choosing. Always a number of the students in this course choose "The Devotional Chapel" as a subject. One year a girl wrote this as part of her theme: "When the procession moves down the aisle, it seems to be led by an Unseen Presence." Why did Epictetus, being "a reasonable creature . . . praise God"? Why did the girl at DePauw University write of "an Unseen Presence"? Must they not, centuries apart, have had a similar vision? Would there were always that Unseen Presence at our services of worship.

Bishop Francis J. McConnell tells a story of a group of fishermen from their village on the Newfoundland coast who went daily to the banks in their fishing boats, returning to their homes in the evening. On one occasion, driven home early by a severe storm, all but one old man, a greatly revered member of the community, made port safely. When but a short distance from shore his boat was driven on a rock and completely wrecked. But he was able to reach the rock and to cling to it. It was impossible for his friends to rescue him; to have attempted it would have been suicide. A large fire was built on the beach; and all through the night, by turns, the men on shore stood in the light of the fire waving their caps in order that their friend might see them and know that, even though they could not *do* anything, they could let him know that he was not forgotten—that he was still loved by his comrades and that they had not deserted him.

We cannot *do* anything for God in return for His goodness to men other than to strive earnestly to do His will and to show Him our gratitude and appreciation by singing His praises, by giving thanks to Him for His great mercy, by standing publicly to bear witness of our love and devotion. If we can do nothing more, these may be acts of deepest reverence, homage, and devotion. Of such things true worship consists.

Since I am a reasonable creature it is my duty to praise God. This is my business; I do it; nor will I ever desert this post as long as it is vouchsafed to me; and I exhort you to join in the same song.

II

WHAT IS A HYMN?

THERE WILL BE QUITE GENERAL AGREEMENT WITH THE statement that Charles Wesley was the greatest writer of hymns the world has ever known. Neither in output nor content has anyone exceeded or excelled him. Hymns numbering upwards of sixty-five hundred he wrote for any and all occasions. The last words addressed to him by his father seemed to stay with him throughout his life and to act as the supreme guiding force of that life: "Be steady, Charles, be steady. The Christian faith will surely revive in this kingdom. You shall see it, though I shall not." In the Prologue to *Charles Wesley, Evangelist and Poet* F. Luke Wiseman said:

To the revival of that Christian faith, to its exposition, its proclamation, its exemplification, its expression, he gave himself with the fervor of a prophet and the lyrical passion of a psalmist.[1]

Earlier in this same Prologue, Dr. Wiseman wrote:

To him it was granted by means of his extraordinary lyrical genius to express the adoration, lead the devotion, inform the mind, enlarge the understanding, quicken the imagination, purify the affection, guide the aspiration, build up the faith, enrich the experience, voice the call, inspire the testimony, provoke the zeal, unify the spirit of the Methodists, not only of his own time but of future generations. Even to-day if one wants to discover or to receive the essential spirit of Methodism or to do its characteristic work, one turns for inspiration not to John Wesley's *Sermons* or to his *Notes on the New Testament*, nor to the Rules of the Society, nor even to usages of the church called by his name, but to Charles Wesley's hymns.[2]

One might well paraphrase the latter part of that extravagant statement and not exaggerate: Even today, if one wants to discover or to be aware of the essential spirit of Christianity or to do its characteristic work, one turns for inspiration, not to the great sermons which have been preached, not to the commentaries on the Scriptures which have been written, not to the dogmas and doctrines of the various denominations which make up the great brotherhood, nor to their usages, but to the hymns of the Church.

> A charge to keep I have,
>   A God to glorify,
> A never-dying soul to save,
>   And fit it for the sky.
>
> To serve the present age,
>   My calling to fulfill;
> O may it all my powers engage
>   To do my Master's will!

Note the first two lines of the second stanza. Hymns have ever been written to serve their age—"the present age"—and preachers and laymen have always had their "calling to fulfill."

Just what is a hymn? A hymn is not a thing subject to rigid definition. In St. Augustine's comment on the footnote which closes the second Book of Psalms, "The prayers [according to the Septuagint, the 'hymns'] of David the son of Jesse are ended," he gives this definition:

Hymns are praises of God with singing, hymns are songs containing praises of God. If there be praise, and not praise of God, it is not a hymn. If there be praise, and praise of God, and it is not sung, it is not a hymn. It is necessary, therefore, if it be a hymn, that it have these three things: both praise, and praise of God, and that it be sung.

In almost the same words he repeats this definition in his comment on Psalm 148. It is an excellent definition; it commends itself as such, and what he says is true in respect of a very large number of hymns. But the definition is inadequate even when taken in its widest sense and meaning. As it stands, it excludes too many of our greatest hymns. For not all of our hymns are hymns of praise: many of them are prayers, others meditations, and still others expressions of personal experience. Judged by St. Augustine's standard alone, many verses which have proven their right to the name "hymn" through having been sung by the Church throughout many generations would be excluded.

His third canon, however, may be accepted without question, for any verse which may not lend itself to singing is, because of that lack, not a hymn.

Arthur E. Gregory, in his *The Hymn-Book of the Modern Church,* commenting on St. Augustine's definition of a hymn, says:

That the primary idea of a hymn is praise may also be granted, but even so "praise" must be given an extensive connotation, that it may include whatever directly or indirectly glorifies God. St. Paul's exhortations show how much more than the offering of adoration is included in the province of Christian song. Our hymn-book, like the Hebrew Psalter, must have not only its songs of high thanksgiving, its sacrifice of praise, but also its prayer of the penitent as he poureth out his soul unto God, its sin-offering as well as its thank-offering, its intercession and meditations, its instructions and exhortations, its lighter songs and melodies.[3]

Nor, Dr. Gregory continues, should St. Augustine's second canon be "regarded as implying that every hymn must be formally addressed to God." [4] Canon John Ellerton said: "Every feeling which enters into any act of true worship may fitly find expression in a hymn." [5] Among our most greatly loved and most helpful ones are examples of devout meditation which do not speak directly to God. Watts's "There is a land of pure delight," the imagery of which was suggested as the young poet of twenty-two sat meditating while looking out over lovely Southampton Water, is but a song; but it has long been included in our best collections of hymns. When one sings it he has a feeling of indirect prayer.

> There is a land of pure delight
>   Where saints immortal reign;
> Infinite day excludes the night,
>   And pleasures banish pain.
> There everlasting spring abides,
>   And never-withering flowers;
> Death, like a narrow sea, divides
>   This heavenly land from ours.
>
> Sweet fields beyond the swelling flood
>   Stand dressed in living green;
> So to the Jews old Canaan stood,
>   While Jordan rolled between.
> Could we but climb where Moses stood,
>   And view the landscape o'er,
> Not Jordan's stream, nor death's cold flood,
>   Should fright us from our shore.

Perhaps this hymn has lost something through the omission of two of its original stanzas:

> But timorous mortals start and shrink
>   To cross this narrow sea,
> And linger shivering on the brink,
>   And fear to launch away.
>
> Oh! could we make our doubts remove,
>   Those gloomy doubts that rise,
> And see the Canaan that we love
>   With unbeclouded eyes.

These are the fourth and fifth stanzas of the original. The first two lines of the original fifth were some of the last words spoken by John Pawson, one of the earliest presidents of the English Conference:

> Oh! could we make our doubts remove,
>   Those gloomy doubts that rise,

and he continued: "Doubts? Gloomy doubts? Where are they? I know nothing of gloomy doubts; I have none. Where are they gone?" It might not be amiss to suggest that there is a crying need for a type of preaching which might aid in dispelling the many doubts which are assailing the minds of many people in this present age.

Another hymn which carries no direct address to God but is a commanding statement of faith, of the imperishable power of the Cross with all of its spiritual implications, an amazing statement of evangelical doctrine made by a Unitarian, is Sir John Bowring's:

> In the cross of Christ I glory,
>   Towering o'er the wrecks of time;

All the light of sacred story
  Gathers round its head sublime.

When the woes of life o'ertake me,
  Hopes deceive, and fears annoy,
Never shall the cross forsake me:
  Lo! it glows with peace and joy.

When the sun of bliss is beaming
  Light and love upon my way,
From the cross the radiance streaming
  Adds more luster to the day.

Bane and blessing, pain and pleasure,
  By the cross are sanctified;
Peace is there, that knows no measure,
  Joys that through all time abide.

In the cross of Christ I glory,
  Towering o'er the wrecks of time;
All the light of sacred story
  Gathers round its head sublime.

Garrett Horder, English authority on hymns, says this "*is* a noble hymn; equally fine in thought, feeling, and expression." While there is no direct address to God, it teems with His presence.

These are hymns which surely come within the limits of Philip Schaff's definition of a hymn as "a spiritual meditation in rhythmical prose or verse." And, just as surely, they meet the final test which any real hymn must pass: It must be of such character as regards both text and tune as to make it suitable for congregational singing. This requirement implies that it must not only read well but sing well.

Much devotional poetry which reads well is not available

as hymnic material for the reason that it does not lend itself to singing—singing, that is, by a group. There is also religious verse that has both these elements of a good hymn and yet fails to have that *life* without which it is ineffective. For if there is no life, there is no feeling; and feeling lies at the heart of all true religious experience. Stating that theological and philosophical formulas follow feeling in importance, William James speaks of it as the "deeper source of religion." Without it religion too often becomes a barren intellectualism and an abstract formalism.

St. Augustine's definition is inadequate. In the directions St. Paul gives for the use of singing in the Church he twice refers to "psalms and hymns and spiritual songs," thus implying that the forms it may assume may be many. This ambiguous word "hymn" has been defined as (or has been spoken of as comparable to) a "sacred lyric," a "song of praise," a "poem in stanzas written to be sung in congregational services," an "extra-Biblical poem of worship, opposed to a psalm"; but definitions culled from dictionaries are not always satisfactory. Nearly every modern hymnbook contains some canticles, some prose psalms set to chants; but most of them are ill-adapted for congregational singing. Perhaps the simplest way to state the case is to say that the present-day Protestant conception of the word "hymn" is that it is a religious poem divided into stanzas which a congregation may sing by repeating the same tune to each stanza. And that, perhaps, is about all that may be said by way of defining the word as Christians use it.

Having established a working definition of a hymn, let us now turn to the consideration of those elements or characteristics which are essential to great ones. However it may be defined, a hymn, to be worthy of the name, must be worthy of use in the worship of the Divine. It must be *sincere*.

> The fineness which a hymn or psalm affords
> Is when the soul unto the lines accords,

says Herbert in "A True Hymn." The thoughts expressed by the poet should be real to the singer. Although he probably could not have expressed them so fittingly, he nevertheless has capacity for understanding them and feeling them. A teacher of philosophy in a Midwestern college was asked one time by his father, a humble farmer with little formal education, just what the son was teaching. After a simple statement as to what was being taught, the father said: "I've been thinking that all of my life, but I couldn't say it." So the religious poet, the hymn writer, comes to our aid and says for us those things which are in our thinking but which we lack the capacity to express. He couches in appropriate language many of the finer religious thoughts which many of us would never be able to utter except through him. We feel a responsibility for expressing our devotion but lack words to do so. The fact is, hymns aid us in making articulate our convictions; they draw out what is already there; it is through their use, in our attempts at expressing ourselves, that we give point to our emotions and clarify our thinking. In a very real way we learn by doing: outgo and income are corelative; expression and impression go hand in hand. As to their use, "there is no part of public worship which calls for more serious and intelligent consideration [and sincerity] than the selection of hymns suited to the occasion and to the congregation." [6]

Are we always sincere when we sing some of our present-day popular hymns? Being sincere is being honest, being free from hypocrisy or dissimulation. Just how sincere are some of us when we sing

> "Are ye able?" said the Master,
> "To be crucified with me?—"

especially the fourth stanza:

> "Are ye able?" Still the Master
> Whispers down eternity,
> And heroic spirits answer
> Now, as then, in Galilee,
>
> "Lord, we are able." [7]

Are we, really, honestly, such "heroic spirits"? An elderly lady, not noted for her piety, who seemed to be greatly enjoying herself while singing this, was asked if she were really sincere in what she had been saying. Apparently surprised, she asked what was meant. When the questioner became quite specific, she replied she had never given thought to the implication of the words: she just liked to sing the tune! Her reply, at least, was honest.

And a hymn must not only be sincere; it must be *reverent*. Many are the instances of irreverence which might be cited, especially in some of the hymns which appeared in the eighteenth and early part of the nineteenth centuries. One writer, in referring to early Moravian hymnbooks, said, "The most characteristic parts of the Moravian hymns are too shocking to be inserted here," while certain details of Christ's crucifixion referred to in some of the Roman Catholic and even Anglican hymns are not only irreverent; they are almost indecent realism.

We do not need, however, to look beyond certain specimens of our former Methodist offerings to find "horrible
examples" of irreverence. In one of the first, probably the
first, of the semiofficial books of hymns issued in this country for the use of Methodists—the book went through at
least two editions, so it must have found some favor among
Methodists—we have some examples. The book, entitled *A
General Selection of the Newest and Most Admired Hymns
and Spiritual Songs Now in Use,* compiled and edited by
one Steth Mead, "preacher of the gospel, M. E. C.," was
published in Richmond, Virginia, in 1807. This particular
hymn has the title "The Experience of a Penitent O-Kellian
Minister, Restored to Methodism."

But five of the thirteen stanzas are given:

Among the smooth Moravians, my parents trained me up,
I liv'd without religion, or grace, or faith, or hope.
They told me Jesus suffer'd for sinners on the tree,
And therefore be contented, you're safe eternally.

They'd preach, and sing, and fiddle, and feast, and sleep, and dream,
But all as soft and tender, as butter, oil or cream;
They'd cry out peace and safety, and told us all was well,
While we were heedless rushing upon the verge of Hell.

The Methodist were preaching like thunder all about,
At length I went amongst them, to hear them groan and shout,
I thought they were distracted, such fools I'd never seen,
They'd stamp and clap and tumble, and roar and cry and scream.

One Spencer was their preacher, whom Satan did disdain,
Hell-fire and damnation he poured like showers of rain;
This rapid Son of Thunder brought me to look around,
And lo! upon the borders of Hell myself I found.

I then applied to Jesus, my wounded soul He heal'd,
With shouts and songs of praises, my mouth he also filled;
This long despis'd confusion I now could freely join,
I told my former brethren, the Methodist are mine.

Other examples, equally irreverent, could easily be cited from the early books of other denominations.

Fortunately, there is little of irreverence in our better hymnbooks today; but there is some of it. A few publishing houses, with less conscience than sense of responsibility, through high-pressure selling methods keep a constant stream of cheap, ordinary, commonplace, inferior books of alleged sacred songs flowing into our churches. Let us not assume, however, that all of the books of this character and all of the poor music and singing are to be found in the country churches. Quite the contrary. It does not necessarily follow that, because New York has its Metropolitan Opera, its fine chamber-music concerts, its excellent church music furnished by such men as Clarence Dickinson, and Chicago its magnificent orchestra and such music as one hears in many of its churches, that all of the music in all of the churches in these cities is to be commended, that it is always the best; for it is not. Just because a city is a great art center, it does not necessarily follow that all of its art is great art. While many of us have seen some of the greatest examples of painting in the galleries in Paris, we have also seen there some of the worst. As a student in Berlin when that city was the unquestioned capital of the music world, this writer heard there more poor music than he has ever heard in any other one place. Not all of it was poor because incompetents were attempting to do something beyond them; it was poor because much of what was being played and sung was poor

music. In the churches of our great cities one may find the
cheapest of cheap books, most of them lacking in those
qualities which should ever be found in books used by Christians in their worship of Almighty God. There is the extreme
opposite to anything reverent in such songs as "I'm gonna
ride upon a cloud and be with Jesus every day," and none
in such well-known ones as "In the Garden."

The note of reverence is dominant in many of our evening
hymns. There seems to be something about the close of day
which makes us want to "stand in awe with admiration."
Could anything be more reverently expressive than such lines
as these by Samuel Longfellow (No. 42):

> O God, our light! to Thee we bow;
>   Within all shadows standest Thou;
> Give deeper calm than night can bring;
>   Give sweeter songs than lips can sing;

the refrain from Mary A. Lathbury's Chautauqua hymn
(No. 44):

> Holy, holy, holy Lord God of Hosts!
> Heaven and earth are full of Thee!
> Heaven and earth are praising Thee,
>   O Lord Most High!

or these four lines from Adelaide A. Procter's hymn beginning, "The shadows of the evening hours" (No. 46):

> Before Thy throne, O Lord of heaven,
>   We kneel at close of day;
> Look on Thy children from on high,
>   And hear us while we pray.

Akin to reverence is *dignity*. In our modern books there

is little which is undignified in the texts of our hymns; most of what there is will be found among the tunes. We still offend somewhat with respect to them. Yet in all fairness it may be said that, with our more thoughtful approach to the organization of our services of worship which has been so marked in recent years, the lighter, more frivolous type of tune is swiftly passing. For with the dignity which characterizes the greater number of our services of worship today, such tunes find little place. Most of them that are still heard are heard in our church schools and in our evening services. With the advent of such excellent books for young people as *The Hymnal for Youth,* issued by the Westminster Press in 1941, we should no longer rely upon the less wholesome "Sunday school songbook" type of compilation with which we have been afflicted for so long.

Hymns should be *beautiful;* mere expressions of piety are not enough. It has been said that Isaac Watts's greatest error was in his excessive concern for what he termed "vulgar capacities." The years have disproved Dr. Johnson's dogmatic assertion that "intercourse between God and the human soul cannot be poetical." His declaration that religious poetry can never be good because "the topics of devotion are few, and being few are universally known; but few as they are they can be made no more," has been fittingly answered by John Keble in an essay reviewing Josiah Conder's *Star of the East:*

How can the topics of devotion be few, when we are taught to make every part of life, every scene in nature, an occasion—in other words, a topic of devotion? It might as well be said that connubial love is an unfit subject for poetry, as being incapable of novelty, because, after all, it is only ringing the changes upon one simple affection, which every one understands. . . .

> "There's not a bonnie flower that springs
>   By fountain, shaw, or green;
> There's not a bonnie bird that sings
>   But minds me of my Jean."

Why need we fear to extend this most beautiful and natural sentiment to "the intercourse between the human soul and its Maker."

The quotation from Burns which Keble uses doubtless inspired the latter's own lines (part of the closing stanza of his hymn for the Third Sunday in Lent):

> There's not a strain to Memory dear
>   Nor flower in classic grove,
> There's not a sweet note warbled here,
>   But minds us of Thy love.

Above all, hymns should be *simply expressed*. Was it not Tennyson who referred to a great man as being "in his simplicity sublime"? In his excellent article, "What Makes a Good Hymn?" which appeared in the June 10, 1942, number of *The Christian Century*, John Haynes Holmes, no mean hymn writer himself, said that a hymn

must contain not the lightest suggestion of complexity, of either thought or expression. There must be no unusual words, no fanciful figures of speech, no elaboration of diction or of phrase. Those very devices of eloquence and beauty, which the poet commands as the composer commands the instruments of his orchestra, are here quite out of place. Simplicity is the word—simplicity which is the handmaid of clarity. A good hymn must be as clear on the first reading as the second, and as obvious in its essence to the child as to the adult mind.

Because it is not as clear on the first reading as on the second, the hymn of George A. Gordon (No. 78) beginning,

"O Will of God beneath our life," is not a good hymn, notwithstanding its lofty thought and scholarly expression. Somewhat of the same criticism may be made concerning the beloved Dean Tillett's hymn (No. 117), which begins, "O Son of God incarnate." Both are too involved; they require too much explaining. The best hymns are those made up of short words, with a large proportion of monosyllables.

Charles Wesley was a real offender with respect to his use of polysyllabic words. Here we find at least one reason for the nonuse of his hymn beginning, "Father of Jesus Christ, my Lord" (No. 203). Such lines as "Self-desperate, I believe" and "Laughs at impossibilities" are difficult to sing. The second stanza of his well-known hymn beginning, "O Thou who camest from above," has been omitted from many hymnals because of the struggles congregations have had in overcoming such successions of syllables as are found in the word "in-ex-tin-guish-a-ble." In *The Methodist Hymnal* now in general use the stanza was retained because of the statement Charles Wesley made to his friend Samuel Bradburn that his "experience might almost at any time be found" in the first two stanzas of this hymn; it was felt the hymn would, on that account, be of special interest to Methodists.

How different was his use of words in his greatest of hymns, "Jesus, Lover of my soul," whose simplicity is almost unique. Of the 188 words used in the four stanzas found in our hymnal, 157 are words of one syllable; only 31 are polysyllabic, and of these only the words "defenseless" and "unrighteousness" have more than two syllables each. In the extraordinary third stanza there are only 3 words which are not monosyllabic.

And so it was with Isaac Watts in his classic rendering

of the first part of Psalm 90, "O God, our help in ages past."
In the five stanzas (No. 533) selected from the original nine
he uses 113 words, only 21 of which consist of more than one
syllable and 17 of which are of but two; only the words
"eternal" (which he uses twice), "sufficient," and "everlasting" have more. In his last stanza, considered by many to be
the most overwhelming of them all, of the 25 words used
only 2 have more than one syllable. Not always are simple
things great, but great things are always simple.

To the elements which should constitute a hymn—sin-
cerity, reverence, dignity, beauty, and simplicity—there
should be added that of *truth*. It should not be necessary to
elaborate upon or stress this point, for "great is Truth, and
mighty above all things." [8]

Let us return to Paul's letter to the Colossians (3:16),
where he says: "Let the word of Christ dwell in you richly in all wisdom; teaching and admonishing one another
in psalms and hymns and spiritual songs, singing with
grace in your hearts to the Lord." Yet St. Augustine and
others who have given us definitions of the word "hymn" seem
to have forgotten Paul's statement of the purpose of singing
in the early church, namely, "teaching and admonishing one
another." He implies that a hymn has a teaching function,
that there is in it that which will make for mutual edification and encouragement. Add to the teaching function that
of exhortation—"exhorting" is but another word for "admonishing"—and one has said about all that need to be said
concerning effective preaching; for to preach is to proclaim
the gospel, to exhort, to teach, to instruct, or inform by
public utterance. Consideration of the possibilities of the
hymn as a means of imparting Christian ideals has not yet

entered sufficiently into the thinking of the leaders of Christian thought; at least, it is not apparent at this time and in this country.

Reference is not made to the formal, didactic, preaching sort of hymn which was so popular with Isaac Watts and among his followers and imitators; for such hymns have largely disappeared, although some of the hymns of Watts which were written especially to be sung at the conclusion of a particular sermon have survived and may be found in all of our best modern hymnals. Reference is made to those which voice the experience, "not of an age, but for all time," those hymns which emphasize the fact that the worshiper belongs to a mighty body of Christians who are seeking to bring in the Kingdom of God by doing the will of God.

Hymns do have a teaching function. A preacher is a teacher. Next to the Bible, the hymnal is the preacher's finest textbook; a teacher should be familiar with the textbooks he uses.

> Life of ages, richly poured,
>   Love of God, unspent and free,
> Flowing in the prophet's word
>   And the people's liberty;
>
> Breathing in the thinker's creed;
>   Pulsing in the hero's blood;
> Nerving simplest thought and deed;
>   Freshening time with truth and good;
>
> Consecrating art and song,
>   Holy book and pilgrim track;
> Hurling floods of tyrant wrong,
>   From the sacred limits back—

HYMNS IN THE LIVES OF MEN

Life of ages, richly poured,
  Love of God, unspent and free,
Flow still in the prophet's word
  And the people's liberty!

III

PAGAN SOURCES?

THE PRECEDING CHAPTER DEALT, LARGELY, WITH THE PROB-
lem of finding a proper definition for the word hymn—that
is, of defining it in the sense in which Christians use the word.

However, the word hymn is not the sole property of
Christians. We read of the hymns of ancient Egypt, of the
Vedas (the "hymns" to the gods of the early Aryans, the
ancestors of the inhabitants of modern India), of Sumerian
hymns, of those of Assyria and Babylonia, and of the hymns
of ancient Greece. The Romans apparently did not have a
native word for "hymn," but the Greek word was adopted
by the early Christians. Of course, when we refer to Latin
hymns we mean those of the early Christian Church, not
those of the Roman people. The Romans were great organ-
izers; they gave us the foundation for our modern laws;
they developed a fine literature. But, aside from ethics, there
is little, if any, of religio-spiritual significance in their writings.

In the sense of religious songs in praise of the gods, hymns
have belonged to all early peoples. James Moffatt has said
that the literature of an ancient race commonly opens with
songs and poetry. From earliest recorded times men have expressed their hopes and fears, their aspirations and desires in
religious poetry—in hymnic form, we might say. For there

was no force in the life of ancient man which so pervaded his every activity as did his religion.

In primitive stages religion was not concerned with morals as we understand morality today; the earliest morals were nothing more or less than social morals, than common folk customs which more often than not had no superhuman sanction, which had nothing to do with gods or religion. Nature made the first impression on the mind of primitive man, and the powers of nature were interpreted by him to be religious powers. Worshipers did not think of their gods as being interested in right or wrong: they thought only of the might of their gods; hence nearly all of their hymns were sung in connection with propitiatory offerings.

Without any relationship existing between them, all early cultures passed through similar stages of development. Analagies may be drawn in all fields. When the early Spanish explorers reached our Southwest, they found pottery bearing designs exactly like those common to the earliest Greek specimens found in the city of Mycenae. There is such a thing as "cultural immigration"; and it should not be inferred, because of similar development in thought patterns as between primitive peoples, that anyone is the originator of the common idea. Just as children go through similar stages in their development, so have nations and peoples been evolving similar cultures ever since the first dawning of civilizations.

The evolution of musical instruments may be reviewed by way of illustration. While musical instruments may be counted, in their various types, by the hundreds, they may be readily reduced to three quite distinct types, namely, those of the drum, the pipe, and the lyre. These three types represent the three stages which all primitive music has passed through, and the stages occur in the order named. There is no exception to this. Not only is this true; these three types are akin to the three fundamental elements which comprise what we speak of as music—a combination of rhythm, melody, and harmony. The first stage, that of the drum, is that of rhythm; the pipe stage that of melody; the lyre stage, the most complex of all, that of harmony. All of the instruments of the drum type are instruments of percussion, among them being drums of all kinds, rattles, cymbals, gongs, triangles, castanets, tambourines—in short, instruments for marking time. Flutes, single and double reeds, all brass instruments—those upon which but one tone at a time may be played—belong to the pipe class. The stringed instruments in all their varieties—the piano, organ, and all instruments upon which two or more tones may be played simultaneously—constitute the third or lyre group. "As in the geological history of the globe the chalk is never found below the oolite, nor the oolite below the coal, so in the musical history of mankind is the lyre stage never found to precede the pipe stage, nor the pipe stage to precede the drum stage." [1] Among savage peoples we frequently find the drum alone; but if they have the pipe they also have the drum, and if they have the lyre they invariably have both of the others.

In the very lowest order of mankind we find some few peoples who have no musical instruments at all, among them the Veddas of Ceylon and the aborigines found in Tierra del Fuego. On the first rung of the ladder of civilization we have certain Australian tribes, the Eskimos, and some tribes found in Siberia, who have only drums as their instruments; but, as we ascend the ladder, we discover the pipe in the possession of such peoples as the Polynesians and the North and South American Indians, with whom the drum is never found wanting. When the lyre appears among the Dyaks of Borneo, the Finns, the Tartars, and others, as well as the nations of history, both pipe and drum are always present. We have no evidence at all of there ever having been any communication between these peoples, widely separated as they were—no passing on from one to another of any invention or discovery. The only explanation seems to lie in the cultural immigration theory: that men have certain common experiences, that there are certain common sources, just as there are common folk customs. The phrase "cultural immigration" is not a happy one even though it is used by anthropologists. It seems to imply what it is not—a passing on of a phase of culture from one group to another. While I do not like it, I do not know of a better way to say what I want to say.

If the cultural-immigration theory be true in the case of the two arts mentioned, namely, pottery decoration and music, it may well hold true of poetry. Inasmuch as there are those who would have us believe the ancient Hebrew poets found the inspiration for their writing in that of earlier peoples, it would follow that we would have to look to those earlier sources for the roots of our present-day hymnody, granting that our present-day hymnody has evolved from the psalms and other Hebraic lyric writings. It is the purpose of this chapter to look into some of those earlier sources to see if in them we can find suggestions for Christian hymns.

It is true that "the past cannot be eliminated"; it is also true that we find similarity of thought and, in some instances, similarity of expression between pagan hymns and Christian hymns. The oft-quoted Ikhnaton Hymn to Aton, for instance, is highly emotional; but it contains no teaching of social morality and hardly any theology. In fact, much, if not all, of the "social morality" we find in such offerings appears to be read into them. For the more expert the authority, the more of a specialist in his field, the more anxious he becomes to make his case. Being determined to do so, he is inclined to read into things and situations that which is not there. It is not amiss for us to remind ourselves occasionally that a specialist is one who knows more and more about less and less. While there may be and frequently are striking analogies between pagan and Christian hymns, it does not necessarily follow that one is the prototype of the other.

Egyptian literature has a considerable body of religious poems called hymns, but its quality cannot compare with its quantity. These so-called hymns are the reflection of the definitely stereotyped attitude of the Egyptians toward their many gods which is in direct and quite noticeable contrast to the purely personal and genuine expression of the Hebrew or of the Christian. Imitated over and over again to the point of satiety, these official odes, sanctioned by the priests, were used almost without exception for sacramental purposes.

There seems to have been a definite pattern for all Egyptian hymns. It was necessary that the writer refer to the Two Countries (Upper and Lower Egypt) as showing honor to the god, to state that all lands feared him, that he had been successful in overcoming his enemies, that he had the approval of his father, that all of the other gods praised him, that all creatures were glad to join in adoration of his beauty and might, and so forth. All that was necessary to make it apply to any god was to mention his name and possibly refer to some myth which was associated with him. They are all very much alike.

Occasionally there appears, as might be expected in such a voluminous output, a real poetic sense and a certain amount of religious feeling of the type which usually reacts to beauty in any form. The hymn to Re (or Ra), the Sun-god, though stilted, is an example of the best hymns which the Egyptians produced:

Homage to thee, O thou who art Ra when thou risest and Tum when thou settest! Thou risest, thou risest, thou shinest, thou shinest, thou who art the king of the gods. . . . Thou didst create the earth, thou didst fashion man, thou didst make the watery abyss of the sky, thou didst form the Nile, thou didst create the deep, and thou dost give light unto all that therein is. . . . Thou art unknown, and no tongue is worthy to declare thy likeness: only thou thyself. . . . Millions of years have gone over the world, I cannot tell the number of those through which thou hast passed. Thou didst pass over and travel through spaces requiring millions and hundreds of thousands of years: thou passeth through them in peace, and thou steerest thy way across the watery abyss to the place which thou lovest. This thou doest in one little moment of time, and thou dost sink down, and dost make an end of the hours.[2]

The quotation is only a part of the hymn; its tedious repetition of platitudes becomes very wearisome. Adolf Erman, who seems to have been as fair as any of the writers on the literature of ancient Egypt, says:

These [many] hymns to the sun are found in a hundred variations for the morning and for the evening—as a rule they give us more satisfaction than the "adorations" to other gods, probably because the rising and setting of this mighty life-giving luminary awakens in man deeper and truer feelings than a figure of Osiris, or a representation of Ptah. [Though not one of the oldest gods, Ptah was an important one. He was the vivifying intellectual force, honored especially in Memphis. Represented in human form, he sometimes appeared as a pigmy or embryo.] The same may be said of the hymns of Nile; the flowing stream laden with blessing is a visible sacred being, and when the Egyptian treats of the real, and describes the things he daily sees, his art always succeeds the best. This is plainly to be seen in these poems; if we ever find that a pleasing passage has made its way into the monotonous phrases, we may wager ten to one that it has been called forth by some mention of nature.[3]

One would expect that whatever religious feeling the early Egyptians had might find expression in their hymns addressed to Osiris, for he was their most-loved god; there seemed to be a human sympathy between Osiris and his worshipers which was not evidenced in their relations with other gods.

Osiris, nature god, had his counterpart among the local gods of western Asia, where men worshiped Tammuz, or Adonis. Believed to have lived, died, and risen again, Osiris, according to one myth, floated ashore dead on the Phoenician coast, where he was found by Isis inside a green tree. (In the great festival which grew out of this story a fallen tree was replanted—and thus restored to life—then decorated, with singing and dancing. Perhaps we have here the basis for our present May Day festivities.)

But the hymns in honor of Osiris are quite disappointing, as this one will show:

Praise to thee, Osiris, son of Nût, who wearest the horns, and who dost lean upon a high pillar; to whom the crown was given, and joy before the nine gods. . . . Great in power in Rosetta, a lord of might in Ehnas, a lord of strength in Tenent. Great of appearance in Abydos . . . before whom the great ones might be feared; before whom the great ones rose up upon their mats. . . . To whom Upper and Lower Egypt come bowing down, because his fear is so great and his might so powerful. . . .[4]

To the ancient Egyptian this doubtless was meaningful; to us it is nothing but words, mere platitudes, meaningless bombast.

"Beyond this this priestly poet could find nothing to say of this most human of all the Egyptian gods," says Erman in his *Egyptian Religions*.

All of the objective descriptions, as well as the references to the myths and allusions to the mythical incidents, are external to the life of the worshiper. Even the Ikhnaton Hymn to Aton already referred to, which stands almost by itself because of its many points of excellence, cannot, except by a good deal of exercise of one's imagination be conceived of as inspiring even a small part of the 104th psalm. A comparison of lines of the two compositions shows the weakest kind of evidence for the support of the claim that the Egyptian poem was the basis for the psalm.

NIGHT AND MAN

Sun Hymn	*Psalm 104:20*
When thou settest in the western horizon of the sky,	Thou makest darkness, and it is night,
The earth is in darkness like death.	Wherein all the beasts of the forest creep forth.
They sleep in their chambers,	
Their heads are wrapped up,	
Their nostrils are stopped,	
And none seeth the other,	
While all their things are stolen,	
Which are under their heads,	
And they know it not.	

NIGHT AND ANIMALS

Sun Hymn

Every lion cometh forth from
his den,
All serpents they sing,
Darkness broods,
The world is in silence,
He that made them resteth in
his horizon.

Psalm 104:21

The young lions roar after their
prey,
And seek their food from God.

DAY AND MAN

Sun Hymn

Bright is the earth when thou
risest in the horizon;
When thou shinest as Aton by
day
Thou drivest away the darkness.
When thou sendest forth thy
rays,
The Two Lands (Egypt) are in
daily festivity.
Men waken and stand upon
their feet
When thou hast raised them up.
Their limbs bathed, they take
their clothing,
Their arms uplifted in adora-
tion to thy dawning,
Then in all the world they do
their work.[5]

Psalm 104:22-23

The sun ariseth, they gather
themselves together,
And lay them down in their
dens.
Man goeth forth unto his work
And to his labour until the evening.

Nor does it follow because four of the psalms make reference to the protection afforded "under the shadow of thy
wings" that reference is made to the Egyptian goddess Maat,
who may be identified by means of her wings.

While he refers to hymns as a "more lofty style of lyric poetry," Erman says "this branch of poetic art contains nothing very pleasing." Egyptologists cannot find much to say in praise of the Egyptian *Book of the Dead*, admitting it is but a "charm book" containing spells which are believed to be efficacious in securing physical comfort for the deceased and in providing for his material needs.

Granting that the ancient Hebrews were influenced by their life in Egypt, that the literary forms of the Egyptian hymns are couplets showing parallelism in thought and arrangement of words, the familiar style of the old Hebrew poets, we shall have to look elsewhere than to the hymns of ancient Egypt to find any basis for our Christian hymnody; it simply is not there.

"What can be more tedious than the Veda, and yet what can be more interesting, if once we know that it is the first word spoken by the Aryan man," says Ralph T. Griffith.[6]

"Veda" is from the Sanskrit *vid*—"know"—kindred to the Latin root *vid* and the English "to wit"—that is, "to have knowledge." In general form the Vedas are lyric poetry and contain the songs with which the Hindu people, at the dawn of their existence, extolled heroic deeds, praised their gods, and sang of whatever might stimulate their emotional fervor.[7] The Brahmans apply the term to their whole body of ancient literature; but, strictly speaking, the word denotes four collections of "hymns," the majority being lyric verse, namely:

Rig-Veda means "rich knowledge," or hymns of praise. ("Rich" before V becomes *rig*, from a Sanskrit root meaning "to celebrate.") It is the Veda par excellence in the estimation of the student of history; for it is the earliest in point of time and contains all that has been saved from the ancient, sacred, and popular poetry of ancient India. Made for its own sake, not for the sake of any sacrificial performance, it is generally the most interesting, some of the hymns being Indo-Iranian rather than Hindu, and representing the condition of the Aryans before their final settlement in India.

Yajur-Veda, the book of sacrifices—*yajur* coming from *yaj*, "sacrifice"—contains formulas and lines to be uttered by the priest at the various sacrificial ceremonies.

Sama-Veda has to do with the ceremonies attendant upon the brewing and imbibing of the intoxicating drink *soma*. It was after reading the Sama-Veda that Whittier wrote the poem "The Brewing of Soma," from which is taken his great hymn beginning,

> Dear Lord and Father of mankind,
> Forgive our foolish ways.

Atharva-Veda, the "charm" or magic book, sometimes called the Cursing-Veda because it contains so much in the nature of calling for the destruction of enemies.

These four are considered to be of divine origin and to have existed from all eternity, the sacred poets being merely inspired seers who "saw," or received them from the Supreme Creator. They were supposed to have been handed down by word of mouth from generation to generation.

It is impossible to fix, with anything approaching certainty, their dates. The word "history" has no corresponding expression in the Sanskrit; the Hindu mind has never been concerned with past facts based on evidence. It has been said that Hindu writers "framed their chronology, like their geography and astronomy, out of their own heads. It was as easy to write a *crore* of years (ten million) as a century, and the former sounded more marvelous." [8]

There is no date known with certainty in India until the time of Chandragupta, about 300 B.C.; the date of Kāli-dāsa, greatest of Indian poets, long a speculation within a period of a thousand years, is still doubtful to the extent of a century or two. In addition, nothing is known concerning the lives of Indian writers.

Two things, seemingly, were the cause: (1) early India never made any history, never went through war struggles to gain freedom and maintain life such as would make for political development; (2) the Brahmans early embraced the doctrine that all action and existence are evil and therefore felt little inclination, if any, to record historical events. Max Müller, a recognized authority, estimates that the Vedas were composed, as we have them now, about 1500 B.C.[9] Definite dates do not begin to appear in Sanskrit literary history until about A.D. 500.[10] Material things, such as the mere writing of history, have never concerned the Hindu; time and things of earth are of small account. With him the spirit is reality, and the only life worth while is living for the spirit. Such thinking produced a number of moral leaders; and, as might be expected, certain moral pronouncements were made which, perhaps, have been unduly magnified. For instance, Brian Brown intimates that the Hindus were among the first peoples to say anything about the brotherhood of 'man.[11] Nanak, founder of the Sikh religion, said, "God will not ask man what race he is. He will ask him, What have you done?" (We find somewhat similar expressions among the Egyptians.) In the light of India's subsequent history and the present-day condition of its people, a question may be raised as to how efficacious such pronouncements really were. True, there is much of ethical value in the hymns of the Rig-Veda, and mankind should not let die those contributions of the past which forecast progress in human living, nor will mankind willingly do so.

When, in the social development of the early Aryans, the institution of the family was the basis of their society, the father, as its head, offered up all prayers and directed all exercises of worship. From this phase of their social and religious organization, these people gradually came under the control of a body of priests known as the Brahmans, who came to place Vedic thought and interpretation upon a philosophic basis. The Brahmans, becoming all-powerful, eventually made various anthologies from the Vedas, selecting such passages as best suited their purpose. Here we have something comparable to the action of the later leaders of the Christian Church in their summary treatment of the late medieval *Proses,* or *Sequences,* of which more later.

The principal one of these anthologies is known as the Brahmanas—"belonging to the Brahmans"—which contains details of the Vedic ceremonies and is written in prose, being the only genuine prose work which Sanskrit as a popular language has produced.[12]

The Upanishads, concerning which we hear so much, are the philosophical chapters of the Brahmanas and do not concern us directly, as do neither the Yajur-, the Sama,- nor the Atharva-Vedas. If there is anything hymnlike in character in the Vedas it will be found in the Rig-Veda, yet there is nothing there which might be compared with the sublime beauty of the poetry of ancient Israel.

Known as the "Thousand and One Hymns," the Rig-Veda really contains 1028, in some ten books or *Mandalas.* It is difficult to arrive at the exact number, for, while about

150 of them are of later date than the rest of the collection and can scarcely be described as "hymns," a goodly number of those which seem to be single hymns are, in fact, small collections. Counted thus, they number between 1300 and 1400.

In the standards of religious thought and poetical expression which had been developing for several centuries, the Vedic poets felt themselves to be the most recent leaders; in some of the earliest parts of the Rig-Veda, the poets speak of fashioning "new" hymns. After the clans had become settled in their new homes, however, and their religious worship stereotyped, the hymns used in the worship of their gods needed no additions; veneration for the old ones took the place of the joy found in creating new ones. This gave a highly intellectual caste a new interest, that of antiquarian and philosophical research.[13] What a commentary on contemporary attitudes!

The collected remains of the work of many centuries, the Rig-Veda is a library and a literature rather than a book. This is not the place, nor would it serve our purpose, to attempt to give an adequate account of its contents or to discuss the many interpretations which have been placed upon them. It is not the work of primitive or uncivilized men. The early Aryans had inherited a rich culture from their predecessors, and they wished to widen it and extend it for those who would follow them. Professional students had dealt for generations with religious thought and its forms of expression; the Vedic poets belonged to this succession; they had inherited a language adequate for poetic expression; they had followed religious and scientific trends, and prided themselves on their early contributions.

If the earliest hymns of the Rig-Veda were to be collected in one volume, in bulk and general appearance it would be similar to an English metrical version of the Book of Psalms. In the later period of its development it ceases to consist of hymns of worship and becomes a more or less dramatic account of the lives of divine and semidivine beings. Professor H. H. Wilson says that, except in their rhythm and in a few rare passages, they are singularly prosaic for such an early pastoral expression.[14] Their value lies not in their fancy or poetic structure but in their facts, social and religious; the greatest interest in them is historical rather than poetical. Perhaps their worst fault is their interminable monotony.

Composed in various meters, some of the hymns are very simple, while others are quite complex and elaborate. Two or more meters are frequently found in the same hymn— one, for instance (in Book I), showing nine distinct varieties in the same number of stanzas. The meters of the lyric verse are similar to those in which more modern hymns are composed, with their variation of "long," "common," "short," and "peculiar" meters. A stanza usually consists of four lines, and its character depends upon their length. While the most common lines of the modern meters contain six to eight syllables, the Rig-Veda lyric verse usually contains eight to twelve. While being an exception in its translated form, this hymn "To Agni," the deity of sacrificial fire, will show how stanzas may alternate as to metrical form:

To Agni
Bright-gleaming warrior lord,
   Protect us in the fray
From this dense devilish heathen horde
   And all that scheme to slay.

They plot us harm the live-long night,
"Their gods are naught," they boast;
Strike, Agni, hard, nor spare thy might
To wreck the perjured host.

It will be noted the first stanza was "short," the second "common" meter; such alternation continues through the remaining four stanzas of the lyric, which has been rendered into metric verse in the manner in which Isaac Watts and others made metrical versions of the Psalms.

As in their form, so also in their content they resemble, in some respects, the Psalms. It is true, they are composed in honor of many different deities and are, therefore, lacking in unity and force they might have were they addressed to one. But, in common with the Psalms, they are, to an extent, national in character (or at least they reflect the national characteristics of their authors); they emphasize the majesty of the universe; and they exalt the dignity of acts of worship and sacrifice.

A striking difference, however, is shown in their lack of expressions of love and gratitude in the hymns: the worshiper seems, all too often, to be trying to bargain with his god.[15] "I give thee this for that," they imply. Indra, the god characterized by his fondness for war and the soma juice, is informed: "Be thou no trafficker with us; do not give sparingly, nor demand too much." Again, "As at a stipulated price, let us exchange force and vigor; O Indra! give me and I shall give thee; bring me, and I shall bring thee." [16] One could quote at length, but it should not be necessary, nor would there be any point in doing so.

After reading many of the Vedas, the Christian will agree heartily with Dr. K. S. Macdonald:

One thing is very clear to every reader of the Veda, that the desires of the hymnists were ever toward cows, horses, offspring (sons), long life on earth, victory over their earthly enemies, etc.; that the requests for spiritual blessings, or an inheritance in heaven, or immortality, were very few in number, and not very clearly expressed. The visible and sensible, as far as their hopes and wishes were concerned, occupied their thoughts almost to the complete exclusion of the invisible and the spiritual.

Again, we shall have to look elsewhere for the basis of our Christian hymnody.

Some three thousand years before Christ there grew up in the lower valley of the Euphrates a civilization known as the Sumerian, and a little later, to the north, one known as the Akkadian. These peoples, the Sumerians and the Akkadians, in the course of time were merged into what became known as Babylonia. Assyria, in turn, conquered Babylonia, and, as history records, was herself overcome by the New Babylonians, or Chaldeans. This is a very meager and sketchy outline of events covering many generations in that area, but it should suffice for our purpose.

In many respects these peoples, jointly, had developed a civilization comparable to that of Egypt, the principal difference being that the civilization of Egypt was an isolated one, growing by and out of itself and not being colored by foreign influence. "Babylonia, on the other hand, was open on all sides to the incursion of ideas as well as of armies." [17] From the great Chaldean legacies left in the libraries of baked clay tablets covered by cuneiform writings, which in recent years have added so much to our knowledge of these ancient peoples, we have discovered they, too, had developed a considerable hymnody which does not differ materially either in form or content from those of other ancient peoples of whom we know more. They praise their gods, sing of their might, and pay tribute to the glory of their temples. But we find something more here than we have found either in the hymns of the Egyptians or in the Vedas: a germ of that spirituality which characterized the writings of the ancient Hebrews.

That the Hebrews came late upon the field of history, that Hebrew culture was greatly influenced by, if it did not derive from, that of Chaldea is now generally agreed upon by scholars. Taking over, as they did, the lands and cities of the peoples they successively conquered, the Hebrews took over also, in a variety of forms, a culture superior to their own. They found a highly developed language which lent itself to the creation of literary forms which appealed to them; they found an elaborate religious ceremonial which, at times, contained elements of religious aspiration and fervor, and in which hymns and prayers were used—hymns which offered praise to a deity in a place of worship.

In these hymns they found what became the principal features of Hebrew poetry: "the rhythm, the uniform length of lines, parallelism, arrangement in strophes, the rhetorical question, the refrain, the antiphonal responses." [18] These the Hebrews did not invent; they found such literary forms already in existence. They also found a hymnic phraseology which they put to use, and certain basic religious ideas which they adopted. But, again, it does not follow that because they took over certain phases of the culture of the older peoples that they rested there. So far as hymnody was concerned, they created quite a new and distinct type of hymnic expression, one that began and ended with "the exhortation to praise Yahwe," and by power of expression and beauty, simplicity and variety, created some of the greatest examples to be found in all literature. They may nave borrowed a form; but they used that form merely as a vehicle for a new, vital, spiritual expression. Whatever basic conceptions of a deity the Hebrews took over, their genius refined and exalted.

In all old Asiatic religions:

The more human the god, the more divine his nature, and, *mutatis mutandis,* the more human the system of theology, the more divine its origin. The ancient Sumerians felt that, in order to understand their woes and afflictions, their sufferings and needs, their ambitions and aspirations, their god had to be endowed with all the qualities and frailties of human nature. To understand and have sympathy with man *God must be man.* For the Sumerians, therefore, God is "man."

Man does not speak or think of God except in terms of human language and modes of human thought. The more primitive man is, the simpler and cruder will be his conception of God, and, *vice versa,* the more advanced his intelligence, the nobler and more spirit-realized will be his ideas about God. But whatever the ultimate picture of God which man may or may not portray in his mind, the process of reasoning is always the same: it is a process from the "known to the unknown." The human quality is "man." Hence all attributes inherent in man—be they good or bad—man will, more or less, ascribe to his god. The Sumerian god appears, therefore, not only as "gracious, loving, pardoning," but also as "angry, furious," yes, even as "inimical, and hostile." He can "walk," "ride," "lie down," and "sleep"; he can "speak," "eat," "drink"; can "rejoice," "weep," and "make merry."

Not only did the Sumerians ascribe to their gods all possible human attributes and functions, they went further; they transferred . . . even their own *social institutions and functions;* "divine society" came to be the exact reflex of "human society," etc., including all classes of people: male, female, servants of all kinds, all kinds of professions, laborers, etc. The gods as "revealers" reveal what man has previously ascribed to them.

The difference between the Sumerian and the Old Testament

religion is this: according to the Old Testament, "man is the image of God," (Gen. 1:27); according to the Sumerian conception, "god is the image of man." [19]

And here we find the great distinction.

We have only a few examples of a once extensive Assyrian literature; between sixty and seventy Assyrian hymns have been "copied, transliterated, and translated" by Assyriologists.

Nevertheless sufficient literature exists to justify two general observations. The first is this, that the closest correspondence between Assyrian and Hebrew religious poetry is to be found in the psalms of lamentation and supplication, which represent and express only the lowest level of religious experience in the Hebrew psalms. The second general observation is that while Hebrew religious poetry develops, and clearly differentiates into independent literary species, the Assyrian religious poetry does not achieve so full a development, nor so clear a differentiation. The one explanation of this fact would seem to be that Assyrian religion did not go so far in emancipating itself from superstition and formalism, and in achieving a lofty conception of deity and a profound religious experience. Certain it is that Assyria did not develop to the same degree as did Israel the independent prayer of thanksgiving, the independent psalm of faith, the independent wisdom psalm, nor the independent hymn of praise.[20]

Of the three classes of Assyrian hymns—namely, introductions to prayers or magical ceremonies, those where the prayers are unimportant, and independent hymns—the first class, wordy and repetitious incantations, constitutes a large majority. Some ten "Penitential Psalms," "litanies," lamentations, prostrations, and so on, are the most significant in that whatever of spirituality there is will be found here. The "litanies to the gods," just mentioned, are litanies only in so far as they repeat a few words after each address, as:

To my god I have uttered the spell and yet I bear the sin.
To my goddess I have uttered the spell and yet I bear the sin.
To the god and goddess of my city I have uttered the spell and yet I bear the sin.
To the four streets I have uttered the spell and yet I bear the sin.

And so on. Others, so called, are not litanies at all; they are merely other and additional directions for sacrifice and for ritualistic practices.

Much more might be said, but it would be merely repetitious and monotonous, as the hymns of these ancients have been found to be. The more one compares the writings of the ancient Hebrews with those of other ancient peoples, unless his point of view is too humanistic to see what is really spiritual in the Psalms, the more he becomes aware of certain things: among them, that the Israelites had a moral sense, a social sense, a sense of guilt (sin), and an assurance of pardon that no other early peoples had. The Hebrew of old had his feet upon the ground and, while recognizing material values, succeeded in linking up the whole with a conception of higher things.

There were common forms of expression among all Eastern peoples; all had hymns of sorts; there is nothing particularly distinctive in that. But what kind? That is the question.

Perhaps a word should be said about the legacy ancient Greece has left us in the Homeric hymns, yet they were so often addressed to the gods and goddesses who exemplified the very worst human traits that we cannot conceive of them as having in any way influenced our Christian hymnody. The music to which all Greek lyric verse was sung was merely a sort of recitation—not a melody as we understand it. Of harmony in the modern sense, they knew nothing. The Greek was more interested in beauty of form than beauty of sound; hence his most effective, as well as his highest, medium of expression was that of sculpture.

The Romans scarcely associated music with whatever religion they had, music to them being nothing more than a sensual pleasure and an adjunct and ornament to their social life.

It is not until we come to the religion of the Hebrews that we find a praise of God at all worthy of Him.

Philip Schaff, erudite ecclesiastical historian and enthusiastic hymnodist, says in his *History of the Christian Church:*

The Church inherited the Psalter from the Synagogue and has used it in all ages as an inexhaustible treasury of devotion. The Psalter is truly Catholic in its spirit and aim; it springs from the deep fountains of the human heart in its secret communication with God, and gives classic expression to the religious experience of all men in every age and tongue. . . . Nothing like it can be found in all the poetry of heathendom.

And with that statement of Dr. Schaff's we shall say no more about the "hymns" of the other ancient peoples, although there is much more by way of comparison which might well be said.

IV

THE PSALMS

THE BOOK OF PSALMS HAS FIGURED LARGELY IN THE WOR-
ship of all peoples who have acknowledged Almighty God as
their Sovereign Lord since the days of the old Temple worship.
Through all the centuries it has been an inexhaustible source
of spiritual strength and a treasure house of devotion for
the individual as well as for the Church. It has repeatedly
been referred to as the "hymnbook of the second Temple,"
but A. F. Kirkpatrick insists it does not have the appearance of
a collection of hymns for liturgical purposes alone and tells
us that there is no evidence that it was so used in its entirety
by the Hebrews before the Christian era. Doubtless many
of the psalms were written expressly for use in public worship; but, also, many quite evidently were not written with
such a purpose in mind and only by accommodation could
they be so used.

The collection was made not primarily for liturgical purposes but to gather together what religious poetry was in
existence so that it might be preserved, and to provide a
book for use in both public and private devotions. It is remarkable that the "first hymn," a triumphant battle song
ascribed to Moses and sung by Miriam to the accompaniment
of her timbrel; Deborah's great patriotic outburst; and the
purely personal thanksgiving song of Hannah—that foretaste
of the *Magnificat*—were not included in the collection which

was called the Psalms. They could have no place in either public or private devotions, so they found no place there.

Bishop Perowne has said that no other book of Scripture, not even among those of the New Testament, has taken such a hold on the heart of all Christians as has the Book of Psalms.

Calvin said: "All griefs, sorrows, fears, doubts, hopes, cares, and anxieties, in short all those tumultuous agitations wherewith the minds of men are wont to be tossed— the Holy Spirit hath here represented to the life."

The spiritual life of the Church could be written with reference to its use of the Psalms. Many, not all of them, were used in the Temple services and in those of the synagogue; that they were well known in the Apostolic age is evidenced by the quotations from them and the references to them found in the New Testament; the spiritual life of the Master was nourished upon them; they were introduced by way of antiphonal singing into the first Christian church at Antioch; the early Church fathers were extravagant in their praise of them as they were sung; the monasteries and nunneries rang with the sound of their singing; they formed a large part of the elementary liturgies of the canonical hours; St. Ambrose used them in the service which may still be heard in Milan; the Psalms have always had their place in the mass of the Eastern as well as the Western churches; they had their part in the Lutheran Reformation at Wittenberg as well as in that of Calvin in Switzerland and France; they were heard in the Wesleyan Revival in England and in the Great Awakening in America; they have been translated into all languages and are known around the earth. The influence of the Psalms in all times of religious awakenings has been amazing.

The Psalter was the first book of the Bible to appear in printed form. When, by decree of the Council of Toulouse (1229), the Bible was forbidden to the laity, a special exception was made in the case of the Psalms. Because there is so much of the spirit of devotion to be found in it, the Psalter is frequently bound with the New Testament.

Since the organization of the *Book of Common Prayer* for the Church of England in 1549, the second year of the reign of Edward VI, the Psalms have been chanted in the services of that Church, not in any metrical form, but in the prose. With the Ordinal and the Thirty-nine Articles, the Psalter is always bound with the Prayer Book, although, strictly speaking, it is not a part of it. It is interesting to note that the translation of the Psalter found in the Prayer Book is not that of the Authorized Version but that of the earlier version of Tyndale and Coverdale, known as the "Great Bible." It is also interesting to note that when the Prayer Book was revised in 1662 it was deemed wise to retain the "Great Bible" version because of its being familiar to the people. In our contemporary hymnals we have included some of the psalms among the chants, but they have become so well known by their Latin titles that we are prone to forget that they are psalms.

Influenced by the practice of the State Church, non-Conformist bodies in England chant the Psalms, although not so successfully as it is done in the Mother Church. In the nonliturgical churches in America it is not done to any great extent; yet there is now, in certain places, evidence of a desire to introduce the chanting of some of the psalms and canticles into our Orders of Worship.

Perhaps it may not be amiss at this point to say something about this matter of chanting, for we have a considerable number of chants included in most of our modern books. Why are they there? Are we expected to use them? Why not? It has been said that chanting is "an exercise which is very easy in theory and very difficult in practice." Chanting is not as difficult as we have been led to believe, and we should not allow ourselves to be prejudiced against it because of our lack of familiarity with this type of sacred song. There is such a thing as limited experience, and inferences drawn from limited experiences are not always sound. Also, there are persons who seem to have a talent for deducing hastily formed conclusions from tenuous premises. An individual accustomed all of his life to a service whose musical elements consisted wholly of the singing of hymns by the choir and congregation, an anthem by the choir, or a solo or other special musical offering, together with instrumental numbers such as the prelude, offertory, or postlude, would look upon any other form of musical expression—chanting, if you will —as a novelty. Especially would this prove true if he were expected to participate in the novel innovation: he would not like it, never having done anything of the kind before; he would think it not devotional and wonder how others might think it so; it would sound "funny," and he would want it to have no place in the services of worship in his church. *He* does not understand it; *he* is not edified; so he condemns it. Is such an attitude a fair one?

Since *The Hymnary* of the United Church of Canada was issued in 1930, quite a number of other hymnals have appeared in America. An examination of eleven of these new books shows that, of the eleven, three are hymnals for the use of liturgical churches; in them we should naturally expect to find many chants. Seven of the remaining eight have a good selection, the one exception being the new book recently issued by the Joint Commission of the Baptists (Northern Convention) and the Disciples.

Of the seven books referred to, only one has anything to say about how to go about chanting properly, namely, *The Hymnal* of the Presbyterian Church. And what it has to say takes only a few letters more than five lines:

A chant is not a hymn melody to which a text is fitted, but a series of tones to which the words of a psalm or canticle are recited. Chanting is, therefore, rhythmical reading and the words are of prime importance. They should be sung at a uniform rate of speed throughout, with every syllable clearly enunciated; weak syllables should not be slighted, nor strong syllables unduly prolonged.[1]

That is all and it is not very formidable; if we follow such directions we shall find that chanting is not difficult. It is true that chanting has been *made* difficult in the past, for we have been generally following the Anglican style wherever chanting has been attempted in this country.

The Anglican style is based upon that of the old Latin, which had elaborate and minute rules for its proper rendition. This was known as "pointing." Inasmuch as the English Church has never, to this writer's knowledge, put forth any specific rules as to how chants should be pointed, each choirmaster or author of a book on choir procedure and practice has made his own rules. As a by-product, a special technical vocabulary having to do with chanting has been developed.

Such terms as Intonation, the Mediation (or Medial Cadence), the Termination (or Terminal Cadence), the Ferial and Festal responses, have grown out of it.

Technical vocabularies are forbidding things. Just as soon as experts become expert, they seem to make a deliberate effort to impress the novice with their superiority in order to impress him with his inferiority. Now, the Intonation (which, it should be said, is not now generally used) is simply a short introduction; the Mediation (or Medial Cadence) the middle part; and the Termination (or Terminal Cadence), naturally, the close. Ferial use is music for occasions marked by no special observance. Festal use is music of more elaborate character for feast days. So all that it amounts to is that we begin, we sing a few words, and we stop, the melody (or tune) being carried either by the tenors or by the sopranos.

Happily, in our new books, we have done away with technical directions and print the words of the psalms and canticles under the notes to which they are to be sung and let it go at that. The old prejudices against chanting are breaking down, apparently, and it is just as well that this is so; for, as has been hinted, there are indications that chanting may again come into its own. There is now, for instance, in many churches, quite an interest being shown in the proper use of the *Gloria in Excelsis* in the Communion Service; and many of our churches chant the Offertory Sentence:

> All things come of Thee, O Lord,
> And of Thine own have we given Thee.

There is not the slightest chance that our Protestant non-liturgical churches will become interested in doing very

66

much chanting, for the very good reason that we have no place in our ordinary Orders of Service for the use of chants. Yet there seems to be no good reason why the *Venite* might not be used, especially near the opening of the service, for the purpose of arousing the members of a congregation to a realization of what they came to church for.

O come, let us sing unto the Lord; let us heartily rejoice in the strength of our salvation. Let us come before His presence with thanksgiving, and show ourselves glad in Him with psalms. For the Lord is a great God and a great King above all gods—

this is a pretty good way to open a service; it has in it that element of praise and adoration which should be present at the opening of all formal services of worship.

We must not expect too much musical content from a chant; it is a liturgical prayer and a liturgical song. A hymn-like effect should not be expected, nor would such an effect be quite suitable. Not that chanting is not capable of musical expression—it simply is not desirable. It is not fair to judge liturgical music by common standards, for it should differ from ordinary religious music, certainly a great deal from secular music.

Choirs can learn to chant even more easily than they can learn to sing Palestrina and Kastalsky properly. Congregations will learn by rote; have the choir sing a few simple chants regularly, and before you know it the people will be joining in—provided, of course, it is indicated on the printed Orders that they are supposed to join with the choir in the singing. The most important thing about chanting is that the words of the psalms and canticles be committed to memory. Chants cannot be sung at sight as can many hymn tunes. If chanting did nothing else, it might teach our people, our worshiping people, some of the noblest things which have ever been written. What a fine thing it would be could our people be induced to commit to memory the words of the *Venite* (Psalm 95), the *Jubilate Deo* (Psalm 100), the *Bonum Est* (Psalm 92), the *De Profundis* (Psalm 130, which John Wesley heard at St. Paul's on the day of his heart warming), as well as such magnificent canticles as the *Gloria in Excelsis,* the *Te Deum,* the *Nunc Dimittis.*

The *Venite, Exultemus Domino* is Coverdale's rendering of all but the last phrase of the first seven verses of Psalm 95. The last two verses of the chant proper are from other sources. The *Gloria Patri* has been used at the close of the psalms and canticles for many centuries.

The two musical settings in *The Methodist Hymnal* (1935) are from services by William Boyce and John Robinson, respectively. The word "service" in church usage refers to a ritual or liturgical form prescribed for public worship consisting of a series of words and ceremonies. In its musical sense it refers to a full set of musical settings of the psalms, canticles, and other elements participated in by the choir, the congregation, or both, especially in the Anglican Church. None of the metrical hymns or anthems are included. In the "full service" it is usual to write all of the several parts in a common key; hence, they are designated not only by the name of the composer but also by the name of the key in which they are written. Thus we have, in this case, a setting from a service written by William Boyce in the key of *D,* known as *Boyce in D,* and one by John Robinson, written in *F,* known as *Robinson in F.*

Psalm 95 is in two definite parts: the first, used here, is

an invitation to worship; the second, a warning against disobedience. The *Venite* is a twofold Call to Worship: (1) that we may express our gratitude to God; (2) that we may acknowledge His greatness. It has been used as a Call to Worship at least since the time of Athanasius (296?-373), who, in speaking of the services at Constantinople, said: "Before the beginning of their prayers the Christians invite and exhort one another in the words of this Psalm." In the Western Church it has always been used as a prelude to worship; it is a part of the Morning Service of the Church of England; in the Sunday Service of John Wesley, suggested for use by the churches in America, he appoints it to be sung both morning and evening immediately after the sentences following the Lord's Prayer. The great battle hymn of the Knights Templars, it struck terror to the hearts of their foes on the battle fields in Europe and the Holy Land. (No. 626.)

The psalmist was doubtless thinking of the gods of the pagans to whom their worshipers attributed certain virtues when he wrote, "For the Lord is a great God, and a great King above *all gods*." He contrasted them with the Sovereign God, the one supreme object of worship. But we should remember there are other false gods which men worship today: gods of luxury, gods of ease, gods of comfort. The ancient pagans did not have a corner on all idols.

The *Jubilate Deo* ("O be joyful in the Lord") was introduced into the 1552 revision of the Prayer Book as a concession to Puritan demands that some alternative be provided to take the place of the *Benedictus* (Luke 1:68-79) when the latter appeared in some other part of the service. It is the "Great Bible" version of the 100th Psalm made famous through William Kethe's metrical rendering, "All people that on earth do dwell," with its great "Old Hundredth" tune. Except at certain festivals it has been used in the daily service in the synagogue from ancient days. Its place in the Anglican service is following the second lesson. In the John Wesley Sunday Service for the morning it follows the Lesson from the New Testament. (No. 630.)

Shortly before Edward Fitzgerald's death he requested that the phrase, "It is he that hath made us, and not we ourselves," be used as the text to be placed on his tombstone should there be any placed there, remarking that he had never seen this text used in that manner.

While this chant may not lend itself to general use in our services, it might well be given a place in any special thanksgiving Order.

O go your way into His gates with thanksgiving, and into His courts with praise; be thankful unto Him, and speak good of His Name. For the Lord is gracious; His mercy is everlasting; and His truth endureth from generation to generation.

In Wesley's Sunday Service for evening the *Bonum Est* (Psalm 92) is the alternative for the *Jubilate* of the morning. This is the first four verses from the psalm and, as is the case with the others, it is from the "Great Bible." It is not found included in the *Book of Common Prayer* except as appointed for reading on the eighteenth day. The significance of this chant is that here we have opportunity to express real delight in worship, a delight which is not merely acceptable to God but a joy to our own hearts. (No. 634.)

However pleasing and profitable it might be to make further study of the psalms which may be chanted successfully, we are more interested now in those selections from them which have lent themselves particularly to satisfactory metrical rendition. Louis Fitzgerald Benson has said the real foundation of our hymnody was Psalm 100.

Metrical renderings of the psalms have difficulty in preserving much of the "spirit and the glow" of the original, yet in metrical form many of them have doubtless become known to countless Christians who would not have come to know them in their original forms. They are sung by most congregations of professing Christians, and if we look upon these metrical renderings as meditations or commentaries we shall perhaps have a truer conception of what they really are—psalms which have become hymns. Later, further consideration will be given to the metrical psalm.

Many writers have expressed regret that we do not know the circumstances under which some of our most-loved psalms were written, as we know the stories back of such hymns as "Abide with me," "Lead, kindly Light," and "I love to steal awhile away." I believe Bishop Perowne has made a real point, however, in his suggestion that by not knowing too much about the stories back of the writing of the psalms we gain more than we lose. For their unique universality gives them that excellence which has made them appeal to all classes of men throughout the centuries. It has been repeatedly quoted that they were "not of an age, but for all time!"

V

CHANTS AND CANTICLES

LONG BEFORE THE CHURCH OF CHRIST ACTUALLY CAME
into existence, announcement of its coming was made in
song: in Mary's exultant *Magnificat,* in Zacharias' *Benedictus,*
in the primitive form of the *Gloria in Excelsis* as sung by
the angels at Bethlehem, and in the *Nunc Dimittis,* that
soul-stirring song of Simeon. By the time The Gospel According to St. Luke had been written, if not before, this
distinctive Christian hymnody had begun, even though, in
form, it was the culmination of the old Hebrew psalmody
rather than the first fruits of a new art. These early forms
and similar expressions of poetic inspiration found in the
Apocalypse seem to have served as the model for later and
further developments in providing music for worship, bridg-
ing the gap between the older psalms and the early Christian
metrical hymnody. It is significant that these hymns of the
Nativity have retained their place in books of praise throughout the life of the Church; they will be found in most of
the hymnals placed in the pews of our churches, both liturgical and nonliturgical. As they are chanted, that is, in their
musical content, they form a sort of link between the psalm
(or hymn) tune and the anthem—not so well adapted to
congregational singing as the former, yet much better than
the latter.

As to the derivation of our early Christian music, three

hypotheses have been advanced by scholars: (1) that it was a by-product of the new faith; (2) that it was a holdover from the old synagogue service; and (3) that it was borrowed from the Greeks. (1) It would be presumption to assume that the first songs of the Christians were sung in an entirely new idiom. One does not change his manner of speech over night as a result of his conversion; if a man uses incorrect English on the eve of his conversion, it is unlikely he will speak correctly on the morning after. (2) Early converts, except for a few in the very early days, were, for the greater part, Gentiles, not Jews; it is reasonable to assume they were not familiar with the songs of the synagogue.

(3) On the other hand, they were familiar with the music of the Greeks; they spoke their language; Greek culture was their only culture; their other art expressions were but adaptations from the art of Greece. The rude paintings in the catacombs show this: Orpheus taming the wild beasts was modified slightly to represent Daniel in the lions' den; Arion and the dolphin can scarcely be distinguished from Jonah and the whale; Hermes carrying the goat was the model for the Good Shepherd carrying the lamb home on his shoulder. Are we justified in assuming greater independence in the matter of the early believers' music?

While there are no musical documents of the period extant, we do have convincing evidence to sustain the contention that the effective music in the early Church was of Greek origin: Pliny, the Younger, relates that the early Christians sang "to Christ as to a god"; Philo, at Alexandria, said the Therapeutae and Essenes, two sects converted to Christianity by the Apostles, accompanied their songs with a sort of dancing, pointing to a connection with the early Greek drama; near the close of the second century Clement of Alexandria forbade the use by Christians of the chromatic tone series of the Greek system but said nothing of the others. While its form was doubtless that of the older Greek, the earliest Christian music was certainly expressed with an entirely new and different spirit. As has been intimated, there is lack of agreement as to its source; but the most reliable evidence seems to favor the case for Greek music. Whatever it may have been, there is no question about the use of song in early Christian worship.

The "Song of Songs," as the *Magnificat* (Luke 1:46-55) is called, has been used at Vespers in the Western Church since the Middle Ages, but in the Church of the East it is sung with the Morning Canticles. For discernible reasons, the *Magnificat* does not lend itself readily to metrical treatment, and such attempts as have been made so to treat it have been used sparingly. While later versifiers have been somewhat more successful than was Miles Coverdale in his rendering for his *Goostly Psalms and Spiritualle Songes,* none of their offerings have found their way into our modern hymnals. Nor have hymn writers found in this scriptural passage that which would furnish the urge needed to set them at the task of writing verse.

John Telford thinks that, of the three great Nativity hymns preserved for us by St. Luke, this "is the noblest of all," [1] while Bernard Shaw says it is the most revolutionary song ever sung. Mary, the village maiden who sang it, knew what oppression meant. In her day much of the world was dominated by Rome, and her particular part of it suffered severely under the evil rule of King Herod. She knew through bitter experience what it meant to be hungry, and cold, and burdened, and oppressed. And when there came to her "the mysterious foreshadowing of a strange deliverance," she lifted up her heart and voice in song. She praised God for what He is, for what He does, and trusted Him for what He would do. The song is one of praise, humility, and faith; yet it breathes defiance. It took courage in her day and in her place to say: "He hath put down the mighty from their seat, and hath exalted the humble and meek. He hath filled the hungry with good things, and the rich He hath sent empty away." Despite the fact that it is known to most free church members only in its prose-chant form, it continues to keep its place in our hymnals. (No. 632.)

The *Benedictus,* the song of Zacharias (Luke 1:68-79) in which he rejoices at the arrival of the time of the Messiah, was described in a rubric in one of the editions of the first Prayer Book as a "Thanksgiving for the performances of God's promises." It has been used in liturgical worship since the ninth century, at least. (No. 628.)

The original form of the *Gloria in Excelsis Deo,* the "Song of the Angels"—"Glory to God in the highest, and on earth peace, good will toward men"—is found in Luke 2:14. We do not know the details of its first use at Christian gatherings, but it early found favor for liturgical use and was incorporated into the Liturgy of St. James, the earliest of the groups of liturgies receiving the sanction of the Christian Church, either East or West. Here it was directed that it be recited by the priest at the "sealing of the gifts." With slight changes, the gradually expanded elaborate form in which we know it now dates from the fourth century certainly, and possibly from the second. Translated from the Greek into the Latin, it was sung during the sixth century on Sundays and on certain festivals, and came into general use in the eleventh. Known as the "Greater Doxology" and as the "Angelic Song," it has been largely confined to the Western Church and has found no favor in the East except by the Nestorians. Many echoes of it are found in such Christmas hymns as that by Bishop Leigh R. Brewer (No. 99), with its refrain,

> "Glory to God in the highest,"
> The angels' song resounds,
> "Glory to God in the highest!"

and in the old French carol (No. 108), *"Gloria in excelsis Deo!"* However, the *Gloria in Excelsis* is dearer to the hearts of millions of Christians because of its long-continued use in the Communion Service than for any other reason.

The late Dean Peter C. Lutkin lamented that this canticle did not have a better tune than the one in common use and expressed the hope that a more fitting one might be found. Because of familiarity and long use it will doubtless continue to be sung to the Old Scottish Chant, which has a sturdiness and vigor to it that has endeared it to millions of worshipers during the generations it has been used. A matter for more serious concern should be the correction of the printer's error which has obtained for so long. A few compilers of hymnals have been brave enough to omit verse five, thus correcting the error, but most of them have not.

This chant has always been a part of the Communion Service, although, at times, in certain denominations, its use has been optional, and its accompanying rubric always stipulates that it may be either "said or sung." Dr. Nolan B. Harmon reports that Bishop Cooke, in his *History of the Ritual,* declares that if this prayer is to be said it should be said by all; if sung, then sung by all. "But it is more in harmony with the first Communion service to sing the *Gloria in Excelsis* than to say it." "No Liturgy in the world comes to a more solemn or majestic conclusion. All the grandeur and magnificence of language is put into it . . . and it is fitting that all who have partaken of the holy institution should sing their gratitude in this peerless Hymn of the Universal Church." [2]

There is an evident trend in our churches to have the *Gloria in Excelsis* chanted by the choirs, with little encouragement given the members of the congregations to join in the singing. This is a mistake, for it not only violates the rubric but denies the communicant the privilege of expressing his "gratitude in this peerless Hymn of the Universal Church." (No. 588.)

An interesting incident concerning the use of the *Gloria in Excelsis*, related by Christopher Columbus in his diary, was its dramatic singing by the crews of his three vessels when land in the Western Hemisphere was first thought to have been sighted on the evening of September 25, 1492. Thus did American history open with the singing of a Christian hymn.

"Lord, now lettest Thou Thy servant depart in peace. . . . For mine eyes have seen Thy salvation," the *Nunc Dimittis*, the beautiful, tender, pathetic song of Simeon (Luke 2:29-32), came into liturgical use at Compline in very early days and into the Prayer Book in 1549. Arthur E. Gregory says:

How beautiful . . . is the "Nunc Dimittis" whether sung daily at eventide, or when the day of life is ended and the Lord now letteth His servant depart in peace! It is in Christian usage what the sounding of "The Last Post" is to the British soldier, marking the close of the common day or sounding the last farewell to a comrade whose warfare is accomplished. A petty and prosaic criticism may regard as unreal such adaptations of ancient hymns, though consecrated by many centuries' use, but there is as legitimate a poet's license in devotion as in literature.[3]

Simeon's song, it has been said, was "the greeting of the Old Dispensation to the New"; as did the other canticles, it expresses the serenity and peace which came with the new era. (No. 642.)

Together with the simple form of the "Angelic Song," those of Mary, Zacharias, and Simeon are the only complete hymns in the New Testament unless we except the song of the disciples upon being dismissed by the rulers in Jerusalem, in which we find some paraphrasing of the Second Psalm (Acts 4), and, perhaps, the thirteenth chapter of First Corinthians. Though they have been called archaic and artificial, only a narrow conception of worship would exclude them.

Other hymns having scriptural background were, of course, sung by the early Christians, and, in some form, are sung by Christians today. Among them is the *Tersanctus*, which may be considered the oldest hymn of the Christian Church, having had its nucleus in Isaiah's vision. We find it again in the Book of Revelation; it appears in the Greek and in the Latin; and through the centuries it seems to have gathered around it the extreme of expressions of sanctified devotion. Many of our modern hymns use it either in part or as a whole. (Nos. 584, 585, 1, 44.)

The *Gloria Patri*, called the "Lesser Doxology," has been from earliest times the common doxology of the Church. Until the rise of Arianism only the first part of it, "Glory be to the Father, and to the Son, and to the Holy Ghost," was used, the second part being added later as an answer to those heretics who denied the eternity of the Son of God. (Nos. 569, 570, 571.)

Another, not so familiar among nonliturgical worshipers, is the *Benedicite*, the "Song of the Three Hebrew Children," taken from the Apocrypha. A paraphrase of the Forty-eighth Psalm, it begins: "O all ye works of the Lord, bless ye the Lord." It is used in the *Book of Common Prayer* as an alternative to the *Te Deum*.

Of course, such cries, or responses, as "Amen," "Hosanna," "Alleluia," and "Kyrie Eleison," were heard throughout the service; and in some instances certain of these responses developed into songs themselves. Such was the case of the "Alleluia," which was so expanded in its musical setting that, much later, its music suggested the composition of hymns known as *Sequences,* or *Proses.* And we are quite familiar with the expanded music forms used with the "Amen."

This, perhaps, is as good a place as any which will present itself to say something which should be said concerning the present tendency to overemphasize the use of the Amen.

Sir H. Walfred Davies has said: "An Amen cannot be too good. Sing Amens with finality, full-heartedness, completeness. They are music's chance to embody the great Christian affirmative. In singing an Amen, it is well to think you may never sing another. Put everything into it, recalling St. Paul's saying, 'In Him was yea.'" This does not mean that all of them should be sung fortissimo; one may be very quiet and yet be very direct, positive, and intensely devotional. Most Amens, however, are anything but in accord with Sir Walfred's admonition: they are but sweet, pretty musical cadences; they do not "embody the great Christian affirmative"; they seem apologetic, not final. The appropriateness of singing an Amen after each hymn may well be questioned, for not all hymns call for the use of an Amen. The more we use the Amen, the greater the care which should be exercised in its use. To have it strung out, as it were, by using the device of the covered *n*—"A-men-n-n-n-nnnnnn" —after each hymn, after the Lord's Prayer, and after various versicles used for Responses, detracts from its meaning, purpose, and effectiveness. Such occasions do not call for mere musical sweetness.

> Amen, that is, so let it be.
> Confirm our faith continually
> That we may doubt not, but believe
> That what we ask we shall receive.
> Thus in Thy name and at Thy word
> We say, Amen, O hear us, Lord.

Some ministers—too many—have a custom of paragraphing their pastoral prayers, having the choir sing an Amen after each paragraph. Should this be done, the Amen should be sung quickly, somewhat incisively; it should be made the people's part of the prayer, not considered an opportunity to "pretty things up." One wonders how our nonliturgical Orders of Worship are benefited in any way by such use of the Amen. It appears to be something which does not belong, which is "dragged in" for effect.

There are, of course, times when the two-, three-, four-, five-, six-, seven-, or more-fold Amen is fitting and proper. It is fitting at the close of a formal service; it is impressive *if it is done well.* Haltingly done, its performance gives one anything but a sense of assurance; he is too busy wondering if the singers are really going to make it. A minister should speak gently, yet firmly, to his choirmaster and tell him that if his choir cannot do the Stainer Sevenfold Amen well, it would be better not to attempt it at all. Let it be repeated: a common fault is that Amens are sung too slowly —that is, at the close of the hymns, after Responses, and so on. They should not be hurried, but certainly they should not be dragged. St. Jerome said: "At the end of every public utterance of prayer and praise, the Amen of the people sounded like the murmur of the sea or the voice of thunder, while the hollow idols, and their temples that were empty, did echo and rebound to the Church's Amen, so that their fabrics shaked." No fabrics are shaken when a choir sings, "A-m-e-n-n n-n-n-nnnnnnnnn." (Nos. 619-624.)

In a lecture delivered before the Church Club of New York many years ago, the Reverend Dr. William R. Huntington said the *Te Deum* was the most wonderful of all the sacred songs of Christendom. Enlarging upon that thought, he continued:

The wonder of it is the wonder of variety. No rival composition can compare with the Te Deum in point of range and sweep. None is tangent to the deeper thought of man at so many points. Other hymns may surpass it in the exhibition of this or that phase of feeling, but there is none that combines as this combines all the elements that enter into a Christian's conception of religion. . . . The splendid exultancy of the Magnificat, the tender plaintiveness of the Nunc dimittis, the cosmic harmonies of the Benedicite, the clear, bell-like tone of the song of Zacharias, all seem to find congress and unison in what has been well called *Hymnus Optimus*, the best of hymns.[4]

We know nothing of its composition, although there is now quite general agreement that it was written near the close of the fourth century by Niceta, a missionary bishop of Remesiana, in Dacia. Even though there may be some basis for the contention of some late scholars that the first part of it is of considerably earlier date, the earliest mention of its use liturgically is in the Rule of St. Benedict in the first half of the sixth century. The story that it was improvised by Ambrose and Augustine on the occasion of the baptism of the latter by the former, thrilling as it is, is but a legend; it has no basis in fact.

As a whole, the *Te Deum* is definitely a hymn of the Western Church; the East, insofar as it knows it at all, knows it only in its Latin form, even though, curiously, the first ten of the verses are known in four important Greek manuscripts. This does not prove at all that this first part was once a complete Greek hymn, but it does give rise to interesting speculation.

A simple analysis of this classic (No. 625) shows it consists of three clearly defined parts: the first, a distinct note of praise to God the Father, is an act of worship (vss. 1-13); the second, a hymn to Christ, is an act of faith (vss. 14-21); and a third, a series of petitions made up largely of quotations from the Psalms, is an act of supplication. Throughout it is written in the present tense:

> We praise Thee; . . . we acknowledge Thee. . . .
> Heaven and earth are full of the Majesty of Thy Glory.
> . . . the Apostles praise Thee.
> . . . the Prophets praise Thee.
> . . . Martyrs praise Thee.
> The holy Church throughout all the world doth acknowledge Thee. . . .

Thou art the King of glory. . . .
Thou art the everlasting Son. . . .
We believe that Thou shalt come. . . .
We therefore pray Thee, help Thy servants.
. . . save Thy people. . . .
Govern them and lift them up.
. . . have mercy upon us . . .

A universal, corporate expression to this point, it breaks down, as it were, in the last verse and becomes intensely personal:

. . . in Thee have *I* trusted; let *me* never be confounded.

It is a matter for regret that the *Te Deum* is so seldom heard in our nonliturgical churches except on occasions of festival character when, in some elaborate setting, it is sung by choirs alone. Yet it is difficult to chant as it appears in most of our American hymnals. If some simple rhythmical composition such as *Parry in D,* which is mostly in unison, were provided, the chances of its use might be somewhat enhanced. Perhaps a better suggestion would be to use the *Jackon in F* setting commonly sung by our English brethren; for, while in the Jackson form the canticle is sung in free rhythm, the effect is more that of a very simple, quite melodious anthem than that of pure chant.

Canon Percy Dearmer, with others, has suggested that the *Te Deum* be paragraphed and that the last section be dropped, closing the canticle with the words,

Make them to be numbered with Thy Saints in glory everlasting.

There is little likelihood, however, that such suggestions will be followed, even though the first two sections form a complete hymn and though it is generally agreed the versicles and responses of the third division were added to the original hymn at some later date. It has been used in its complete form too long; it has become too much a part of the spiritual lives of too many people to be changed. Elizabeth R. Charles, gifted woman who wrote "Never further than Thy cross" (No. 146), is reported to have told William T. Stead: "The *Te Deum* with its glorious subjectiveness, its tender humility, and its note of hope, has, perhaps, helped and inspired me through life more than any other hymn."

As has been stated in the case of other canticles, the *Te Deum* has not been made in any metrical, hymnlike form which has taken hold on the Church. Charles Wesley, as have others, tried his hand at it in his little book, *Hymns for Those That Seek and Those That Have Redemption*, 1747; but, great hymnster that he was, the result was not at all satisfactory.

It would be a fine thing if our congregations might learn it: for in it we have not only the whole Christian creed; there is a tradition of more than fifteen hundred years back of it. How desirable it would be to have the entire holy Church throughout all the world join in singing this great hymn of praise and faith and supplication at least once each month!

TE DEUM LAUDAMUS

We praise Thee, O God; we acknowledge Thee to be the Lord.
All the earth doth worship Thee, the Father everlasting.
To Thee all Angels cry aloud, the Heavens and all the Powers therein.
To Thee Cherubim and Seraphim continually do cry.
Holy, Holy, Holy Lord God of Sabaoth;

Heaven and earth are full of the Majesty of Thy Glory.
The glorious company of the Apostles praise Thee.
The goodly fellowship of the Prophets praise Thee.
The noble army of Martyrs praise Thee.
The holy Church throughout all the world doth acknowledge Thee.
The Father of an infinite Majesty;
Thine adorable, true, and only Son;
Also the Holy Ghost, the Comforter.

Thou art the King of Glory, O Christ.
Thou art the everlasting Son of the Father.
When Thou tookest upon Thee to deliver man, Thou didst humble
Thyself to be born of a Virgin.
When Thou hadst overcome the sharpness of death, Thou didst open
the Kingdom of Heaven to all believers.
Thou sittest at the right hand of God in the Glory of the Father.
We believe that Thou shalt come to be our Judge.
We therefore pray Thee, help Thy servants whom Thou hast re-
deemed with Thy precious blood.
Make them to be numbered with Thy Saints in glory everlasting.

O Lord, save Thy people and bless Thine heritage.
Govern them and lift them up forever.
Day by day, we magnify Thee;
And we worship Thy Name ever, world without end.
Vouchsafe, O Lord, to keep us this day without sin.
O Lord, have mercy upon us, have mercy upon us.
O Lord, let Thy mercy be upon us as our trust is in Thee
O Lord, in Thee have I trusted; let me never be confounded.

"Hail, gladdening Light," a very ancient hymn, must have
been known before the organization of the Syrian Liturgy
of St. James; for it was incorporated in it. Ascribed to
Sophronius in the Greek liturgical books, it has for centuries
been in high favor in the Eastern Church and has held
great appeal for Russian composers, most of whom have

tried their hands at making settings for this "Hymn to Sophronius," which lends itself so admirably to musical treatment.

Known as the "Candlelight Hymn" because of its use at the Lighting of the Lamps, it has not had extensive use in the Western Church; in fact, only quite recently has it become generally known among English-speaking peoples, and that by way of special musical arrangements for choir use, sung quite generally by college and high-school concert choir organizations. Its inclusion in modern hymnals is largely due to its historical and antiquarian interest; it would be too much to expect modern churchgoers to become very much interested in such dull and uninteresting music as Sir John Stainer has provided for it. (No. 637.)

Of the many translations of the "Candlelight Hymn," the one by John Keble is most used, and that by Longfellow beginning, "O gladsome light," found in his *Golden Legend*, is the most interesting:

> O gladsome light
> Of the Father Immortal,
> And of the celestial
> Sacred and blessed
> Jesus, our Saviour!
>
> Now to the sunset
> Again hast thou brought us;
> And, seeing the evening
> Twilight, we bless thee,
> Praise thee, adore thee!
>
> Father omnipotent!
> Son, the Life-giver!
> Spirit, the Comforter!

Worthy at all times
Of worship and wonder!

The "light" motif has been widely used by hymn writers. (Nos. 32, 114, 345, 378, 599.) Why should it not have been? Mankind has known no greater boon than the coming of the Light of the World. "Every good gift and every perfect gift is from above, and cometh down from the Father of lights, with whom is no variableness, neither shadow of turning."

VI

EARLY GREEK AND LATIN HYMNS

PRIMITIVE CHRISTIANITY WAS SO VITAL, SO VIVID, SO VIRILE, it must express itself in its own terms regardless of whatever debt it owed past expression. The early Christian ministry was one of enthusiasm rather than of office; and we have the right to assume such a ministry would produce something hymnlike in character, if for no other reason than that of enthusiasm for the new faith. It must not be assumed, however, that anything similar to our familiar modern stanza-hymn was produced for some centuries. Yet, St. Paul tells the Corinthians (I Cor. 14:26), "When ye come together, every one of you hath a *psalm,* hath a doctrine, hath a tongue, hath a revelation, hath an interpretation." Surely some of those who had "come together" must have had something of the poetic instinct; and nothing would have been more natural than for such to have given poetic expression, in the form of the period, to their devout contributions.

In order to emphasize their teaching or for purposes of devotion, writers of the New Testament books frequently quoted fragments from hymns in the manner in which Christian ministers do so today. Reading the New Testament in a search for hymns is an interesting, helpful, and inspiring thing to do. In doing so one also gets impressions as to the form and content of early Christian hymnic expression; the number of them is suggestive of a widespread practice. The *Gloria in Excelsis,* the early form of the *Tersanctus* of the Western Church, and the *Hymnus Angelicus* of the Eastern Church, already referred to, are examples, as are such excerpts as:

Awake thou that sleepest [Eph. 5:14];

Now unto the King eternal, immortal, invisible, the only wise God, be honour and glory for ever and ever [I Tim. 1:17, the basis of our hymn numbered 64];

Worthy is the Lamb that was slain [Rev. 5:12];

Blessing, and glory, and wisdom, and thanksgiving, and honour, and power, and might, be unto our God for ever and ever [Rev. 7:12];

Alleluia: for the Lord God omnipotent reigneth [Rev. 19:6];

the last three furnishing the texts for some of the grandest choruses of Handel's *Messiah* and providing the inspiration for such modern hymnic expression as "Honor and glory, power and salvation" (No. 16).

While poetic improvisation has never been limited to any one time nor confined to any one place, it is worthy of comment here that it had existed among the Greeks from the time of Homer and was familiar to all that part of the Orient which had been influenced by Greek culture. George Dwight Kellogg, erudite head of the department of ancient classics, Union College, in a paper, "The Ancient Art of Poetic Improvisation," read before the Classical Association of the Atlantic States in the spring of 1940, said: "The Greeks of Cilicia and of the regions about Antioch and Tarsus seem to have cultivated the art and become famous." It is he who suggests the "gift of tongues" refers to this practice. But, as Ruth E. Messenger tells us in her excellent Hymn Society paper, "Christian Hymns of the First Three Centuries," "the nature of improvisation is fugitive," arising as it does from individual inspiration which is not recorded and not accurately remembered even though couched in familiar terms. Perhaps this is one explanation of the dearth of examples from the early days of the Church, a circumstance we greatly lament. There must have been much of this sort of thing; for the classic Greek meters were unknown in early Christian Church usage until the fourth century, and the old lyric meters do not appear until the ninth.

As the Church grew, its early Fathers were taxed to defend its tenets, for controversy was rampant. Yet out of this very controversy came the urge to produce hymns. Heresy, at least dissent, has ever stimulated hymn writing, Arius, Notker Balbulus of St. Gall fame, Luther, Watts, the Wesleys, Cardinal Newman with the Tractarian group, Samuel Longfellow and other Unitarians, were all dissenters and, out of their disagreements with things as they were, gave us a vital part of our hymnody. If exception is taken to the statement that these men, or some of them, were dissenters, it is nevertheless true they were dissatisfied with certain situations which existed within the churches during their time; and each set about to the best of his ability and in his own way to find means of righting them.

Gnosticism—that early heresy especially rampant in the second century, that movement toward the fusion of beliefs which differed from those of the early Christians but which bore their impress strongly, which tried to reconcile the prevalent philosophy with religion, which influenced the organization of the early Church by fusing various bodies into a compact whole—had a hymnody which suggested certain things to early Christians. The Syrian scholar, Bardesanes (155-223), author of mystic hymns of Gnostic character which were used by Syrian Christians for two centuries before they were driven out by the more orthodox contributions of Ephraem (307-73?), was, perhaps, the most outstanding exponent of the use of hymns as a means of gaining converts. Evidently Ephraem felt that way about it, for he wrote:

> In the resorts of Bardesanes
> There are songs and melodies.
> For seeing that young persons
> Loved sweet music,
> By the harmony of his songs
> He corrupted their minds.

Bardesanes and his son, Harmonius, had compiled a Gnostic "psalter" containing some 150 hymns.

Meanwhile, to the west, the leaders of the churches of the principal part of the empire were being put to it to combat the new heresy which had arisen, namely, Arianism. Arius, its leader, a deacon of Alexandria, from whom the movement derived its name, had recognized the potency of hymn singing as a means of attracting followers and from the beginning of his crusade had used verses set to popular tunes to further his cause. According to the French scholar Duchesne, the sailors, loafers, dock workers, and other commoners of Alexandria had become familiar with them and loudly sang them, much to the discomfort of the orthodox members of the community. Arius' great opponent, Athanasius, while denouncing such tactics, apparently made no effort to counteract the menace with hymns of his own.

Near the close of the fourth century (398), when Chrysostom became patriarch of Constantinople, the Arians, not allowed the privilege of worshiping within the walls of the city, were permitted to enter it on the evenings of Saturdays, Sundays, and some of the festival days. Congregating at prominent points, they spent the nights in singing their heretical songs, which had refrains much in the style of the modern gospel songs, thereby attracting large crowds and much attention. In order to offset this insidious influence, Chrysostom organized a system of nightly processions with torches, banners, crosses of silver, and other evidences of ceremony. The "true believers" taunted and insulted the Arians; the rival groups clashed; and riots and bloodshed followed. Naturally, this led to the suppression of the singing performances of the Arians; but the custom, with modifications, remained a feature of extra-Church procedure.

Ambrose, we have been told by Augustine, had introduced singing in the style of the Eastern provinces into the Western Church at Milan some dozen years before Chrysostom went to Constantinople; and with this innovation we find the first steps taken toward the definite breaking away in the West from the influence of the East.

Of the three language source groups from which we derive much of our Christian hymnody—namely, Syriac, Greek, and Latin—it is necessary only to say that none of those of Syriac origin have come into use in the West, although a number of them have been rendered into English by such able translators as Horatius Bonar and Mrs. Elizabeth R. Charles.

The earliest example of Greek hymnody still in common use is that one which, in its English rendering, begins "Shepherd of tender youth" (No. 429). Should one compare a literal translation of the Greek, by Clement of Alexandria (150?-220?), with the English of Henry Martin Dexter (1821-90), he would have to admit, frankly, that Dr. Dexter's hymn has in it little of the original. Yet it has real historical interest for us and has a certain deserved popularity. If we look upon this hymn as a sort of connecting link between the second and the twentieth centuries, we shall, perhaps, come near to an appraisal of its real value, which is the teaching of the sometimes forgotten truth that throughout the life of the Church men have felt the urge to express their praise of Jesus Christ in words and singing. Dr. Dexter evidently had this in mind; for he wrote his hymn while preparing a sermon on the text, "Remember the days of old" (Deut. 32:7), the theme of which was "Some prominent characteristics of the early Christians." His purpose was didactic: he had the hymn sung at the service in order that the lesson of his sermon might become fixed in the minds of his hearers.

Clement, a Greek and a converted pagan philosopher, head of the Catechetical School of Alexandria, leading reformer of his day, wrote a number of books exposing the prevalent corrupting influence of paganism, one of which was entitled *The Instructor,* or *The Tutor.* At the close of the book, which presents Christ as the ideal Instructor, Clement appends this hymn, a sort of doxology, lauding and extolling the Master who not only enlightens us but calls us into His Church and unites us unto Himself. It is a hymn of praise and thanksgiving for those who have just been received into the Church family. Insofar as is now known, this is the first primitive hymn which has never been put to any liturgical use. (No. 429.)

Other early Greeks who were Christian poets were Gregory of Nazianzus (fourth century) and Synesius (late fourth and early fifth centuries), Bishop of Ptolemais, of whom Mrs. Browning wrote as "the chief, for all true and natural gifts, of all our Greek poets." Their offerings have been translated but have not come into use in either the Eastern or Western churches. As time went on, however, there developed such an interest in hymn writing, with such an extraordinary output, that, we are told by John M. Neale, the service books of the Greek Church, the "Eastern Breviary," as they have been called, comprise "on a modern computation," some "five thousand closely printed quarto pages in double columns, of which at least four thousand are poetry." It is this collection which supplies the source from which Dr. Neale made his so-called translations which we find in our present-day hymnals.

Before discussing some of these hymns in some detail it might be well to quote from Dr. Neale as to the difficulty which is encountered when one attempts to do Greek canons into English, where he tells us the "perfection of Greek poetry is attained by the Canons at Lauds,"—Lauds being one of the offices of the canonical hours. He says:

In attempting a Greek Canon, from the fact of its being in prose,—(metrical Hymns . . . are unknown,)—one is all at sea. What measure shall we employ? why this more than that? Might we attempt the rhythmical prose of the original, and design it to be chanted? . . . We have no pattern or example of any kind to direct our labour.[1]

Perhaps that is the reason the Western Church knew little or nothing of the wealth of Greek hymnody until Dr. Neale first issued his volume *Hymns of the Eastern Church* in 1862. He began translating in this field in 1850, twelve years before he was induced to publish his little book.

One would like to digress here from his main purpose to pay tribute to this remarkable person, John Mason Neale, one of the greatest classical scholars the world has known. Kind, modest, unassuming, weak physically but strong mentally, a prodigious worker with an indomitable will, he spent the greater part of his adult life at East Grinstead, a miserable market town, some twenty-five miles south of London, whose principal industry was, and is, brick and tile making.

A graduate of Cambridge University, the only preferment he ever held (which was really not an ecclesiastical preferment) was that of warden of Sackville College (which was not a college at all but an endowed old-folks' home), the appointment carrying an annual emolument of some £27, most of which he gave away. At times ignored, at others humiliated, frequently the victim of petty persecution by his immediate ecclesiastical superior, other countries than his own, much to its shame, evinced a sincere appreciation of him and his work, Harvard University conferring on him the degree of Doctor of Divinity, and the Metropolitan of Moscow honoring him by presenting him with a valuable copy of a rare liturgy.

His extreme High-Church views, his sympathy with the Oxford movement, caused him great embarrassment; he suffered vigorous opposition and occasional physical violence. While gentle in manner he "adhered to his principles with iron inflexibility."

Establishing one of the early nursing schools in England,

known as St. Margaret's Sisterhood, he enlarged its scope by founding and adding to it, variously, an orphanage, a middle-class school for girls, and a rescue home for women. All are still flourishing except the rescue home, which had to be abandoned because of local prejudice.

Best known to the world at large as a literary figure, he has been unequalled as a translator of Greek and Latin hymns. His linguistic ability was extraordinary—he knew twenty languages—and he wrote voluminously on a variety of subjects, most of his works being published posthumously. Reading the story of the life of this unusual man should act as a tonic to one who feels his lot has been cast in rough and hard places.

Returning now to the consideration of the Greek hymns which in their English form have established for themselves a prominent and permanent place in our hymnody, we note contributions by St. Anatolius (d. 458), the first poet to emancipate himself from the tyranny of the old laws of literary composition. We know him through the hymn,

> Fierce was the wild billow,
>   Dark was the night;
> Oars labour'd heavily,
>   Foam glimmered white;
> Trembled the mariners,
>   Peril was high:
> Then said the God of God,
>   "Peace! It is I."
>
> Ridge of the mountain wave,
>   Lower thy crest!
> Wail of Euroclydon,
>   Be thou at rest!

Sorrow can never be,
  Darkness must fly,
Where saith the Light of Light,
  "Peace! It is I."

Jesu, Deliverer,
  Come Thou to me;
Soothe Thou my voyaging
  Over Life's sea!
Thou, when the storm of death
  Roars, sweeping by,
Whisper, O Truth of Truth,
  "Peace! It is I."

This hymn, while well known in England and included in the Protestant Episcopal hymnals is this country, is not found in many of our recent American hymnals. It is, perhaps, the best of the hymns of Anatolius—at least of those of his certain authorship. If we accept Dr. Neale's belief that he wrote "The day is past and over," however, that statement may well be questioned.

"The day is past and over" (No. 52) appears in the Late Evening Service of the Orthodox Church and, therefore, usually carries the credit "Anonymous." It is possible that Dr. Neale confused this St. Anatolius with another saint of similar name who lived some centuries later; recent scholars are generally of that opinion. In any event, examples of Greek hymnody of the first three centuries are pitifully few. Others than those we now have may, in time, be rendered into an English which may prove acceptable as well as useful, for recent years have seen a revival of real interest in their further study; but it is unlikely that this generation of hymn singers will become familiar with them. This evening hymn is said by Dr. Neale to be a great favorite in the Greek

Islands; the native melody to which it is sung there is "singularly plaintive and soothing."

Four other Greek hymns, written some three centuries later, which have been made known to us through Dr. Neale are: "Come, ye faithful, raise the strain" (No. 151), "The day of resurrection" (No. 159), "Art thou weary, art thou troubled?" (No. 193), "Christian! dost thou see them?" (No. 275). The third one in the list perhaps should not be included; for, although Dr. Neale included it in the first edition of his *Hymns of the Eastern Church,* in the third edition he said it has so little of the original Greek in it that in future editions he would place it in an appendix. It is, however, one of the great hymns of all time and should continue to have wide use. In order that interesting variety in our use of hymns may be introduced occasionally into our services, this one may be sung antiphonally; or it may be read with effectiveness, the congregation reading the questions and the minister replying with the last two lines of each stanza. (No. 193.)

The other three hymns mentioned are representative of the last group of Greek religious poets who have made any impress on our modern hymnody. These hymns were written during the period of the iconoclastic controversy, that movement which did so much to aggravate the enmity between Eastern and Western Christendom which had been gradually developing during the centuries. As they had been used to combat others, hymns were effective in combating this heresy. One of them, "Christian! dost thou see them?" was a valiant battle cry—and might well be one today. (No. 275.)

The foregoing meager and altogether inadequate account of Greek hymnody does not take into account certain prayers from the ancient liturgies which have been metrically arranged as hymns by some of our modern hymnists. An example of this is the Introit "Let all mortal flesh keep silence," which in its original form is not a hymn at all but a prayer appended to the Cherubic Hymn sung immediately before the "Great Entrance" in the Liturgy of the Church of Jerusalem, commonly known as the Liturgy of St. James. Consisting of four stanzas as rendered into English by Gerald Moultrie, it is frequently included with the Eucharistic hymns in modern books. In others the first stanza alone quite properly is used as an Opening Sentence. (No. 594.)

It is not feasible to attempt to deal altogether chronologically in treating so extensive a subject as that with which we are engaged; there are too many overlapping movements. As the Christian world broadened, these movements became ever more widespread. In order to maintain even slight coherence, one must follow a certain movement through and then return to pick up the beginnings and trace the development of a new one.

Through the still-recurring use of certain Greek phrases, such as *Kyrie eleison*, in modern liturgies, we are reminded that the language of the Western liturgies was Greek, not Latin. Greek was the written language of the Church Fathers and ecclesiastical writers until Tertullian began writing in Latin—not the Latin of literary Rome, but that of the people. Tertullian died about 230, so it is not surprising that we find no Latin hymns until the fourth century. There is record of a book of hymns compiled, perhaps written, by St. Hilary (d. 367?), arch opponent of Arianism who was exiled to Phrygia by the Emperor Constantius; but, as none of these hymns have been found suitable for Western use, we are not concerned with them.

It is to Ambrose (d. 397), already mentioned briefly, that we must return if we would look into the beginnings of that extraordinary list of writers of Latin hymns which were to influence profoundly the entire Western Church until the Lutheran Reformation—hymns many of which are still in common use. Bishop Ambrose of Milan, father of Latin hymnody (incidentally of all Western Church song), untrained as a theologian, became bishop through accident rather than through preferment or design. Following the usual course of education of his day, Ambrose became proficient in Greek, chose the law as his profession, and received a consular appointment which made his residence in Milan a necessity. Having become well and favorably known because of his ability as an orator, when it became necessary to elect a successor to Auxentius, Bishop of Milan, who died only a few months after Ambrose assumed his post there as consul, the latter was elected by acclamation. Presiding at the meeting held in the church for the purpose of electing a new bishop and finding it necessary, because of the excitement caused by the importance of the occasion, to plead with the people to maintain order, Ambrose was forced to accept the office when a voice cried, "Ambrose is bishop," and the cry was enthusiastically taken up by the entire throng.

Scholar, organizer, statesman, in time a great theologian, defender of the Catholic faith against Arianism in the West, he especially concerns us as a poet and a musician. As a poet he began the writing of religious songs for the people and for the congregation in the fullest sense of the term. His verses were popular in content and form; the general cultural level of Milan was high, so a respectable standard was set. As a musician, called "the father of Church song" by Grimm, he introduced the practice of antiphonal chanting in the Western Church and began the systematizing of its music, a task completed by Gregory the Great two centuries later. So effective was the work by Ambrose, he was charged by the Arians with using his hymns to evoke magic spells. This challenge he gladly and proudly accepted, saying: "They allege the people are deceived with the magic spells of my hymns. I do not deny the fact. For what can be more powerful than a confession of the Trinity daily sung by the mouths of a whole people?" And, it may be echoed, what can be more powerful than a singing people? "Let me make the songs of a people and I care not who makes the laws," is an oft-repeated truth. More to the point in our discussion is George Herbert's declaration:

> The Church with psalms *must shout,*
> No door can keep them out: . . .
> Let all the world in every corner sing
> My God and King!

Scholars have experienced perplexity and difficulty in fixing upon hymns which may honestly be credited to Ambrose. One difficulty in definitely identifying them is caused by the excellence of the work of his imitators; each meticulously copied his style. Even the metrical stanza he used (which corresponds to our Long Meter) became so much his own that it became known as the "Ambrosian meter." At the beginning of the seventh century, two hundred years after his death, Isadore of Seville said, "Hymns are from his name called Ambrosian."

In connection with reference to Ambrose' influence on hymnody, however, a word should be said concerning the Spaniard Prudentius (348-410?), even though none of his hymns are now, nor were they ever to any marked extent, in common use. While his hymns appeared much later than those of Ambrose, Prudentius was his contemporary and, like him, a lawyer and public official. Prudentius created a new type of religious poetry; whereas religious poetry had been an official and congregational expression when it had not been liturgical, his was that of personal and domestic edification, not intended for public use. Ambrose was a classicist; Prudentius, in marked contrast, a romanticist. Ambrose wrote in but one meter; Prudentius, imitating Horace—sometimes surpassing him—wrote in a variety of meters. One is reminded of the manner in which Charles Wesley broke away from the conventional forms employed by Isaac Watts and other predecessors some centuries later. Ambrose influenced form, Prudentius content; the one was a restraint, the other a stimulus.

Archbishop Trench says of Prudentius:

He does not attempt as they did (i.e., the older Christian poets) to pour the new wine into old bottles; but has felt and understood that the new thoughts and feelings which Christianity has brought with it must of necessity weave new garments for themselves.

On the other hand, he says there is an "almost austere simplicity which characterizes the hymns of St. Ambrose," and continues:

. Nor do we fail . . . to observe how truly these poems belonged to their time and to the circumstances under which they were produced—how suitably the faith which was in actual conflict with, and was just triumphing over, the powers of this world, found its utterance in hymns such as these, wherein is no softness, perhaps little tenderness; but in place of these a rock-like firmness, the old Roman stoicism transmuted and glorified into that nobler Christian courage, which encountered and at length overcame the world.[2]

In *The Methodist Hymnal* there are two translations of the *"Splendor paternae gloriae"* ("O splendor of God's glory bright")—one of the twelve hymns which have been definitely assigned to Ambrose by the Benedictine editors, the first (No. 38) translated by John Chandler, an Englishman, and Louis FitzGerald Benson, our country's greatest hymnologist, and the second (No. 638) translated by Robert Bridges, late poet laureate of England. The latter is more interesting, not only because it more truly reflects the spirit of the original text, but because of its ancient tune.

In the absence of any example of Prudentius' hymn writing, it perhaps might not be amiss to offer these lines from his *Peri Stephanon*, a book of fourteen poems glorifying the martyred saints:

> Yet has Christ a need of mē,
> Though but a moment's space I have my station;
> Earthen vessel though I be
> I pass into the Palace of Salvation.
>
> Be the service ne'er so slight,
> God owns it. Then, whatever Time is bringing,
> This shall still be my delight.
> That Christ has had the tribute of my singing.

VII

LATER LATIN HYMNS AND SEQUENCES

"THE CHRISTIAN POETS WERE IN HOLY EARNEST," SAYS
Archbishop Trench speaking of the medieval period in his
Sacred Latin Poetry. "The gospel brought into men's hearts
longings after the infinite and the eternal." As has ever been
the case, these longings they strove to express in poetic form
and in so expressing them brought into their poetry that
mystical element which so pervades the whole of the hymn
writing of the Middle Ages.

An interesting study for the student of classic literature
is the tracing of the causes for the breaking away, by these
medieval Christian poets, from the insistence upon the element of quantity rather than accent and rhyme in the poetry
of the time. Doubtless their real concern was for what they
had to say rather than for the manner in which they might
say it. And in that which has come down to us through the
centuries, even though our acquaintance with it be merely
through translation, we find they did a magnificent job.
Something more than form in poetry is necessary if it is to
have continuing interest after it is translated. The fact that
what was said in Latin is so meaningful when translated into
our various modern languages is but further and additional
evidence that the great Christian poets of the Middle Ages
were more interested in content than in form. Which suggests the thought that perhaps a reason why contemporary

poets are making little or no worth-while contributions to our hymnody in this challenging age is that they feel bound to express themselves in those present-day conventional forms which lack the simple, fundamental elements of rythm and rhyme which are so necessary if lyric poetry is to take hold of and make an impression upon the minds of persons of normal artistic appreciation. Our poets seem to be cursed with the worship of one of the idols of our time, the idol of conventionalism. Let us hope that, if any benefits at all come out of our present world-wide conflict, one of them will be the shattering of this idol.

Yes, the early "Christian poets were in holy earnest," were men of zeal, consumed with the desire to spread the glad tidings of the Christian gospel, to teach by any and all means available. Certainly that may honestly be said of the most of them. But, as has been the case in other situations, there crept into the fold at least one who, apparently, had not always been "in holy earnest." Thinking of Venantius Fortunatus one remembers David and recalls some old lines:

> King David and King Solomon
>   Led merry, merry lives,
> With many, many lady friends,
>   And many, many wives;
> But when old age crept over them,
>   With many, many qualms,
> King Solomon wrote the Proverbs
> And King David wrote the Psalms.[1]

Venantius Honorius Clementianus Fortunatus, born about 530 in northeastern Italy, not satisfied with the four names with which he had been christened, took a fifth, Theodosius. The last of the old classic writers, as he became the first of the troubadours, the connecting link between Prudentius and the hymn writers of the later Middle Ages, he was the first of the Christian poets to exalt the worship of the Virgin Mary until it became a passion. Later becoming mere idolatry, Mariolatry remains even today in some of the more backward Roman Catholic countries.

Fortunatus' adoration of Mary doubtless was the result of his infatuation for Queen Radegunde and her maid, Agnes, a story often told and well known. Neither a holy man in the highest sense of that term, nor a very bad one, Fortunatus was a real poet whose hymns live today. Unfortunately, his finest hymn, "*Vexilla Regis prodeunt,*" in translation beginning, "The royal banners forward go," is not found in many present-day hymnals for the very good reason that other desirable ones are not there—lack of space. This is a rich processional hymn for Easter; "its author invites us," Neale says, "to contemplate the mystery of love accomplished on the cross." We do, however, find another of his great hymns in most of our modern hymnals, namely, "Welcome, happy morning" (No. 161). This is one of the renderings of his "*Salve, festa dies*"—"Hail, festival day"—which has been the inspiration for so many so-called "*salve*" hymns.

Another, quite modern in thought and interesting because of its being written in elegiac couplets, the metrical pattern in which Fortunatus cast the original, is "Welcome, day of the Lord" (No. 395), which its author says was written on request. Its first stanza follows quite closely the original:

> Hail thee, Festival Day! blest day that art hallowed forever;
> Day whereon Christ arose, breaking the kingdom of death.

But beyond that it is new. It is fitting for processional use, or it may be equally desirable for use as an opening hymn.

There seems almost cause for regret that there is real doubt as to the authenticity of the story connected with "All glory, laud, and honor," John Mason Neale's translation of the justly famed Palm Sunday processional, *"Gloria, laus et honor,"* composed by Theodulph of Orleans. The story goes that Theodulph, having written the hymn to help him pass away dreary hours while a political prisoner at Angers, was released after King Louis I, called the Pious, walking in procession on Palm Sunday, 821, heard the hymn sung from the cloisters where Theodulph was being held. So impressed was the king by it that he ordered Theodulph restored to his ecclesiastical rank, that of bishop, and decreed that the hymn be sung as a processional on Palm Sunday thereafter. It is even now, more than eleven hundred years after its writing, very generally used on that occasion by all Christian churches, both Protestant and Catholic. It is one of our best Palm Sunday hymns, picturing as it does the homage paid the Master upon His entry into Jerusalem, the only occasion when He received public acclaim. (No. 128.)

Some three hundred years later the most important man of the twelfth century, Bernard of Clairvaux, wrote what Philip Schaff has called "the sweetest and most evangelical hymn of the Middle Ages," the *"Jesu dulcis memoria"* known as the "Joyful Rhythm of St. Bernard on the Name of Jesus." The gospel took on new meaning for Bernard, one of the greatest preachers of all time, when he discovered it was intended to comfort the hearts of human beings. Dealing with fundamental moral questions, he sought to arouse the souls of his hearers, to cheer them, to sustain them; and he urged them to press forward toward the victory which he knew might be in store for them.

There have been other men, Augustine and Luther for instance, who by their words and writings have ploughed deeper and more lasting furrows in the great field of the Church, but probably no man during his lifetime ever exercised a *personal* influence in Christendom equal to his (Bernard's); who was the stayer of popular commotions, the queller of heresies, the umpire between princes and kings, the counsellor of popes, the founder, for so he may be esteemed, of an important religious Order, the author of a crusade. Besides all deeper qualities which would not alone have sufficed to effect all this, he was gifted by nature and grace with the rarest powers of persuasion, and seems to have exercised a wellnigh magical influence upon all those with whom he was brought into contact.[2]

The great hymn of Christ's passion, "O sacred Head now wounded" (No. 141), is ascribed to him, although it comes to us in Dr. James Alexander's translation by way of that of Paul Gerhardt.

This Bernard, however, has won the lasting gratitude of the Church because of his having written the "Joyful Rhythm." Even though his authorship has been questioned— Percy Dearmer says, "It is not by Bernard"—Archbishop Trench quite pertinently asks who did write it if not Bernard. Be that as it may, the Church for several hundred years has thought of it as his and will doubtless go on thinking so. Few Latin hymns have been so often translated by so many different hands. Three renderings of it are in common use. One, "Of Him who did salvation bring," has been used in America since the days of Bishop Asbury. Another, Ray Palmer's much loved "Jesus, Thou Joy of loving hearts!" is perhaps the most popular and the least medieval of the numerous translations. A third translation, by Edward Caswall, vies with Dr. Palmer's rendition for popularity and wide use.

It has been happily married to the lovely tune "St. Agnes," which John Bacchus Dykes wrote for it.

The other Bernard, he of Cluny, although not a hymn writer at all, certainly deserves at least passing notice. He was the author of that "wondrous satire" on the evil conditions of the time in which he lived, the twelfth century, a long poem of some three thousand lines entitled *De contemptu mundi*, and beginning, "*Hora novissima, tempora pessima, sunt: vigilemus.*" Little is known of this Bernard other than that he entered the Abbey of Cluny some time after 1122 and that he spent the remainder of his life in the luxurious establishment which in the twelfth century reached the climax of its reputation. Its church was the grandest in France; the beauty and richness of its ritual has perhaps not been excelled at any other time or place. It was the most extensive and opulent of the many similar establishments then scattered over Europe which had been condemned by Bernard of Clairvaux as places of gross self-indulgence. Contemplating the fearful corruptions of the age, during his leisure moments Bernard wrote his bitter satire, beginning it with a description of heaven, contrasting his conception of what heaven was like with the miserable afflictions under which the people were living and the frightful conditions to which they were subjected.

From the first part of Bernard's long poem Dr. Neale translated 218 lines, out of which he made four hymns: "The world is very evil," "Brief life is here our portion," "For thee, O dear, dear country," and "Jerusalem the golden." Until recently these all were to be found in various hymnals. They were included in the last (1943) edition of *The Hymnal* of the Protestant Episcopal Church; and *The Hym-*

nal of the Presbyterian Church, printing of 1926, carried all but the first, "The world is very evil," while the 1905 edition of *The Methodist Hymnal* had in it the last two, "For thee, O dear, dear country" and "Jerusalem the golden." Evidently the Methodists were the first to discover that the world *is* very evil—perhaps so evil they didn't want to continue singing about it. In all but one of the latest editions of Methodist hymnals the only one of these hymns which has been retained is "Jerusalem the golden" (No. 529).

Those stanzas of "Jerusalem the golden" which are now commonly used are lines of rare beauty which have taken strong hold on the imagination of Christians. While many will agree with John Brownlie's criticism that Bernard was writing of a material heaven in which there was little of the spiritual, perhaps more of us will think of his lines much as did Samuel W. Duffield when he wrote:

So strange and subtle is the charm of this marvelous poem, with its abrupt and startling rhythm, that it affects me even yet, though I have but swept my fingers lightly over a single chord. I seem to myself to have again taken into my hand the old familiar harp, whose strings I have often struck in times of darkness or of depression of soul, and to be tuning it once more to the heavenly harmony which the old monk tried to catch. Perhaps some day, when the clouds are removed, I shall see him, and understand even better than now the glory that lit his lonely cell, and made him feel that

> "Earth looks so little and so low
> When faith shines full and bright." [3]

Of all the Latin hymns now in common use none has been taken to the Church's heart as has the anonymous *"Veni, Creator Spiritus"*—"Come, Holy Ghost, our souls inspire"—

which, used at Pentecostal services a thousand years ago (the earliest recorded occasion of its use was 898), has, in intervening years, been sung at the most impressive and solemn functions in English history as well as at consecrations and ordinations of bishops, elders, and priests. Known to all ministers of the gospel and to millions of laymen, this hymn with its accepted ancient plain song is a treasure of treasures. (No. 636.)

Certain detached Latin hymns such as "My God, I love Thee" (No. 214), ascribed to St. Francis Xavier, and "O come, O come, Immanuel" (No. 83, 1st stanza), the first of the Seven Greater Antiphons which are sung at Vespers in the Anglican Church during Advent, have attained established places in our hymnals.

Late years have shown a renewed interest in the old Latin hymns, and this interest seems to be growing. Dr. Ruth Ellis Messenger has published an excellent treatise on the subject, her dissertation submitted to Columbia University as one of the requirements for the degree of Doctor of Philosophy and published by that institution under the title *Ethical Teachings in the Latin Hymns of Medieval England*. It is worthy of study

The late Canon Percy Dearmer had a marked fondness for these old hymns and has given us some excellent modern ones modeled upon them. Already attention has been called to one of them, "Welcome, day of the Lord." Another, "To the Name that is salvation" (No. 79), is a rendering, in part, of the *Glorioso salvatoris*, fifteenth century, anonymous; but it is very up-to-date in its expression, as will be noted upon reading its last lines.

To many of us, however, one of the most interesting and

significant developments along hymnic lines, principally those prior to the year 1000, was the invention of the Prose, or Sequence, and its derivative, the Trope. It is interesting because of the manner of its creation and development, and significant because it was in the interest of the common worshiper. It is referred to as an invention because that is what it was, nothing more nor less.

In the Roman Mass a respond, called the Gradual, is sung between the reading of the Epistle and the Gospel just as we sing the *Gloria Patri* after the Responsive Reading or between the readings from the Old and the New Testaments, respectively. This particular respond, a psalm called the *responsorium graduale* because of a supposed similarity to the psalms of degrees, Psalms 120-34, which were long thought to have been sung from the steps of the Temple, was similarly sung from the steps leading to the ambo (pulpit) in the church. Originally consisting of an entire psalm, the *psalmus responsorius* (or *responsorium graduale*) in time was shortened in order that the *Alleluia* which followed, and which was sung by the people, might be lengthened. The reason for lengthening the *Allelulia* was a very practical one: to cover the time taken by the deacon in his ascent to the rood loft, where he read the Gospel after having read the Epistle from the steps leading to the choir. The rood loft, or rood-cross, in the old churches was sometimes a pulpitlike box where the elaborate cross was placed. If the church were large, or the deacon old or fat, perhaps with the gout, several seconds would elapse during the journey from the steps to the loft. In order to cover this lapse of time, the last syllable of the *Alleluia* was set to a type of florid song (technically, "melisma"). The *Alleluia* seems to have been introduced sometime during the fourth century by Damasus, Bishop of Rome, following a suggestion by Jerome, who had heard it in a service at Jerusalem. By the sixth century the melismata had been developed, and as time went on they were stretched out to almost unbelievable lengths. It was difficult for the people to remember the long string of notes, as they had to be learned by rote. No intelligible notation was then in existence; the few who could read the music had spent years in the learning. The notes (melisma) following, or part of, the *Alleluia,* were generally called *sequentia;* but the synonymous terms *jubilus, melodia,* and others were also used. It will thus be seen that the word *sequentia* was originally a musical term. Some of the musical figures were so long drawn out that it became necessary to separate them into divisions in order that the singers might find a breathing place. Of course, as the interest in the sequences grew, many were written which were quite too difficult for the common people comprising the congregation to sing, so the performance of them was delegated to the choir.

It seems that some monks at the Abbey of Jumièges, not far from Rouen, had hit upon the device of breaking up these florid passages by setting words to them—one syllable to each note. When, as a result of the Norman invasion, the Abbey of Jumièges was burned, at least one of the members of the establishment, fleeing from the Normans and carrying his service book with him, reached the great monastery of St. Gall. Here the unique treatment of the melismatic passages was noticed by the famous Notker Balbulus (840-912) who at once became aware of its attractive possibilities. Notker, having received much training in poetry and music, was the natural leader at St. Gall; and it fell to his lot to establish what we commonly call a Sequence as to form, and to popularize it. His interest in people and his desire to restore to them, in part at least, their opportunity to participate actively in their worshp, led him to set about writing words to go with this music. Because his first texts, like those from Jumièges, were neither rhythmic, metrical, nor in rhyme, they were properly called Proses. As rhythm, meter, and rhyme gradually asserted themselves these texts became known as Sequences. Eventually there was little, if anything, to distinguish the sequence from the hymn. A story is told to the effect that Notker's first sequence, the *"Media vita in morte sumus"*— "In the midst of life we are in death"—was suggested by his watching some workmen at the dangerous task of building a bridge over a deep chasm. Luther used this sequence in translation as one of his funeral hymns, and all but the opening sentence of that part of the burial service of the Church of England which is used at the grave at the time of internment is taken from it.

Another story told of Notker has interest for us. Impressed by the insistent, continuous sound of a mill wheel, he was moved to compose his sequence on the Holy Spirit, the *"Sancti Spiritus adsit nobis gratia"*—"Present with us ever be the Holy Spirit's grace"—which he sent to the Emperor Charles (the Bald) with his compliments. In return, by the same messenger, so goes the story, the emperor sent Notker the hymn *"Veni Creator,"* which, says Ekehard,[4] the same "Spirit had inspired him" to write. So, if true—and it has an air of truth—we must credit Charles the Bald, the grandson of Charlemagne, with having written it rather than Charlemagne, to whom, although undoubtedly of anonymous authorship, it is frequently attributed.

The "*Sancti Spiritus*" of Notker certainly influenced the writing of the "*Veni, Creator Spiritus*" regardless of the authorship of the latter, and the two have long inspired writers to produce such excellent "Holy Spirit hymns" as John Newton's "May the grace of Christ our Saviour" (No. 27), an excellent benediction hymn; Isaac Watts's "Come, Holy Spirit, heavenly Dove" (No. 172); Samuel Longfellow's "Holy Spirit, Truth divine" (No. 173); Charles Weslew's "Spirit of faith, come down" (No. 183); and the more modern ones "O Spirit of the Living God" (No. 182), by Henry Hallam Tweedy, and "Spirit of Life, in this new dawn" (No. 178), by Earl Marlatt. Notker composed sequences for nearly all of the festivals of the year and published them in a collection which not only held its place in Germany until the Council of Trent but was influential later. In form, content, and musical phrasing Notker's work was entirely original—a practical, musical, and liturgical innovation as great as had been that of Ambrose.

We find many examples of sequences in old English and French "tropers," that is, books of tropes. From some old French sources we find that the natural and appropriate title "*sequentia cum prosa*" (tune with text) was used to designate this peculiar style of sacred song, whence came the two terms Prose and Sequence which are now used without discrimination. While the first is older and more accurate, the second has more general use.

Although the sequence developed through adapting a text to a known melody, because of the varying length of the melismata and of certain restricting rules of literary composition, it was not a great while before interest was aroused in writing texts in the established proper form to which original melodies might be set. Julian lists some nine pages, small-face-6-point type, of titles of sequences appointed for use on various festivals, saints' days, and so forth. Between the eighth and fifteenth centuries some five thousand are said to have been written—quite too many to recognize officially. Finally, at the Council of Trent, it was decided to sanction but four of them for liturgical use, namely: *Victimae paschali*, for Easter; *Veni, Sancte Spiritus*, for Pentecost; *Lauda Sion*, for Corpus Christi; and the *Dies Irae*, for Requiem Masses (masses for the dead). Later, in 1727, the *Stabat Mater dolorosa*, for Good Friday, was admitted.

The *"Victimae paschali,"* in its original form, is an excellent example of what a sequence could be. It has fine rhythm, is in rhyme, is simple and scriptural. It is the parent of such Easter hymns as "Jesus Christ is risen today" (No. 155) and Charles Wesley's "Christ the Lord is risen today" (No. 154).

The *"Veni, Sancte Spiritus,"* called "The Golden Sequence" in the Middle Ages, is almost unknown among English-speaking people outside the Roman and Anglican churches, while the *"Lauda Sion,"* although found in many translations, does not appeal to Protestants. In fact, its use anywhere in public worship has been very limited.

The *"Dies Irae,"* originally for use during Advent, is now the Sequence in the Mass for the Dead. No other sacred Latin lines have been so frequently rendered into English; Julian says there have been more than 150 translations of it made. In older Methodist and other hymnals various renditions of it appeared in that section of the books called "Time and Eternity—Justice and Retribution," or with

116

other titles equally significant. Having lost their fear of retribution, apparently, modern compilers have not seen fit to include any translations of the *"Dies Irae"* in their hymnals.

The *"Stabat Mater dolorosa"* (No. 138), attributed to Jacopone da Todi, who was "a fool for Christ's sake," according to Archbishop Trench, is so decidedly Roman Catholic in spirit, so full of Mariolatry, that only a small portion of it can be used by Protestants. Louis F. Benson has given us a fine translation of that portion, in which he has nicely preserved the literary flavor of the original sequence. The *Stabat Mater* has an unusual appeal for composers of music, some of their finest contributions being their scores provided for its text, while the ancient plain song associated with it is one of the great musical expressions of all time.

Because not every sequence text had its own melody, several texts being written for one and the same tune, in order to identify a particular tune some distinctive title had to be given it. If we except the names of the tunes to which some of the psalms were ordered to be sung, we have here our first instances of giving names to hymn tunes—incidentally, an interesting study in itself.

"Trope" is a collective term used in the liturgico-hymnological sense to designate texts, either prose or poetry, written for the purpose of amplifying and/or embellishing a liturgical text which is in itself complete—for example, *Introit, Kyrie, Sanctus, Gloria,* and so forth. These interpolations which grew out of or were suggested by the sequence, do not in any way change the character or meaning of the official liturgical text but rather amplify, augment, or elucidate it. They are, in a sense, a commentary upon it.

The trope and the sequence (or prose) are closely related, yet they differ fundamentally: while the sequence is an interpolation of the liturgy itself, the trope is not an interpolation of the official text of the liturgy. The sequence is an independent unit in itself; the trope is not, usually being devoid of meaning if set apart by itself. However, as time went on, the original short, pertinent commentary or response (in some cases the antiphonal trope) became expanded into longer lines, a whole stanza, then a series of stanzas, until it grew to be an independent religious folk song. An example of the simple commentary type is that of the *Kyrie* trope (facing No. 575):

> *Kyrie:* Lord, have mercy upon us.
> *Trope:* And incline our hearts to keep this law.

One of the longer type is the Easter hymn beginning, "The strife is o'er," which was patterned after the lovely "*O filii et filiae,*" which is a trope on the *Benedicamus Domino* at the close of the Breviary hours, written by the Franciscan friar Jean Tisserand (d. 1494).

There may be some connection between the trope and the carol; for the dramatic character of some of the Christmas and Easter tropes, as well as those for other seasons, developed until they became little plays of religious character similar to the earlier miracle, mystery, and morality plays of the medieval period.

Tropes are of peculiar interest to the musician, for they represent practically the total musical advance from the ninth to the twelfth centuries. The compositions of the music writers of the period not admitted to the Gregorian service books were gathered up and, forming independent collections, supplemented the official books.

The Council of Trent, about the middle of the sixteenth century, marks the dividing line between the Middle Ages and the more modern period in hymn writing. When liturgy was considered established and complete, there was nothing more to do. Mere commissions to do things do not supply inspiration. That which is manufactured and not the result of growth is only another proof that what has been extinguished—has died out—cannot be brought back to life by a decree. The reason the old Latin hymns deteriorated as they did was that there was no incentive to write them other than that afforded through competition in literary excellence. That is why, in our day, hymns written to be entered in contests are usually failures. And it is also the reason why we are seeking a new form of evangelistic effort —a new technique, to use a much abused word. The old, having served its purpose, has seen its day.

VIII

CHORALES AND METRICAL PSALMS

WHILE MARTIN LUTHER MAY RIGHTFULLY BE CALLED the Father of Protestant hymnody, he did not invent it. Ambrose was the inventor of the metrical hymn, and from his first efforts grew that great body of hymnic material upon which rests that now in use by all Western Christian churches both Roman Catholic and Protestant. Coleridge said, "Luther did as much for the Reformation by his hymns as by his translation of the Bible." His was perhaps an extreme statement, but there is much of truth in it; for hymns certainly were a potent, if secondary, means in making the Lutheran revolt the overwhelming success it turned out to be. Through them the congregational character was given to Protestant worship.

Short vernacular hymns, tropelike in character, were first introduced into Germany in the ninth century, called, after their refrain, "*Kirleison*" (*Kyrie eleison*), or "*Leisen*," or "*Leichen*." One of them is the Easter hymn,

> *Christ ist erstanden,*
> *von der marter all,*
> *des sul wir alle fro sein,*
> *Christ sol unser trost sein,*
> *Kyrie leyson.*

In Miles Coverdale's rendering,

> Christ is now risen agayne
> From his death and all his payne;
> Therefore will we mery be
> And rejoyse with him gladlie.
> Kirieleison.[1]

For congregational use there were also the sequences of Notker and others, some macaronic hymns (a curious mixture of Latin and the vernacular), and others used in connection with the Christmas mystery plays, as well as certain translations of the canticles and psalms. So, when Luther found himself in need of some vehicle for congregational praise he found at hand not only this fund of ecclesiastical and popular song but the established forms of the Hussites and other earlier reformers. Not only had metrical vernacular verse been written, but the custom had arisen among the early Bohemian Brethren of singing these texts to popular melodies. At least one of them, "Innsbruck," is in common use in many denominations today, but it has never found favor among Methodists.

Luther needed new psalms and hymns to take the place of the current Latin ones if he were to have the vernacular public worship he so much desired. While it is true there were many German-language hymns known to the people, most of those of the later medieval period were so tainted with idolatrous references to the Virgin Mary and with hagiolatry as to make them unfit for use by him. He, therefore, confronted with the task of securing new ones, appealed to his friends, among them Spalatin. Writing him in 1523, he said:

It is my plan . . . to make vernacular psalms for the people. . . . We seek therefore everywhere for poets. . . . But I desire that newfangled and courtly expressions may be avoided and that the words may all be exceedingly simple and common such as plain folk may understand, yet withal pure and skillfully handled.

And the following year he wrote:

I wish, after the example of the Prophets and the ancient Fathers of the church, to make German psalms for the people, that is to say, sacred hymns, so that the word of God may dwell among the people by means of song also.

Sensible of Paul's statement about "teaching and admonishing one another," and setting about following it with characteristic German thoroughness, the Lutheran hymns became in large measure didactic and theological. It was partly due to this cause that German hymnody came so soon to deviate from the early definition of Augustine as to what a hymn should be; it embodied a variety of compositions not before considered suitable for Church use. Their success was due partly to their metrical structure, which, while sometimes complicated, was easy and had variety, and to the well-known and popular tunes. The total output of German hymns has been enormous—more than a hundred thousand according to Philip Schaff. Of these, some thousand are of exceptional literary merit; yet for some reason few of them have "taken hold" outside Germany proper, except in the Scandinavian countries. There is something about them which lacks whatever appeal is needed to give them wide use in English-speaking countries, except, of course, where there are numbers of Christians of German ancestry.

The word "chorale," connotatively meaning hymn and tune but used with us as referring to "tune in German style," came into use in the latter part of the sixteenth century and was the peculiar interest of the Evangelical (Lutheran) Church as opposed to the Reformed (non-Lutheran) Church, which body disapproved of hymns, believing them to lack direct inspiration. The chorales, that is, the musical settings of the German hymns, have found more use in England and America than have the hymns themselves. This, perhaps, is due to the insistence of some musical leaders that their musical excellence is such that the Church is the loser by not incorporating them into its sacred song. Be that as it may, it is nevertheless true that they have never been accorded any too generous reception by our people.

One reason why this is true may be that given by Hamilton C. MacDougall when he called attention to the fact that worship music should not be chosen primarily for its cultural value. Music which is called "good" because it answers to quite generally accepted aesthetic standards may not in any way meet the equally relevant standards of music for services of worship. There should be no belittling the use of the very best in music, or the best in anything and everything else, for that matter, in the worship of Almighty God. But, while the great vernacular hymns of Luther were an expression of fellowship in worship, it was a fellowship which was distinctly racial and, in large measure, national. Worship, as D. H. Hislop stressed in his Kerr Lectures, 1935, should always be expressed in terms which are universal. The tunes which were sung to these hymns were as definitely racial as were the texts of the hymns themselves. Many of them are universal in their musical appeal, but by far the majority of them are not. Some things are timeless—"universal," we say—in their appeal: the sayings of Jesus, for instance; things which are common to all times and to all men. So with this German music: parts of *The Messiah, Ein' feste Burg,* and some other compositions are universal; but not all. Further, in Germany the words of a given hymn are always associated with a given tune, no other ever being used; the music suggests a specific text, which is all to the good. Perhaps the taking of the chorales from their original texts and applying them to others may be another reason why they have not been able to withstand transplanting. With few exceptions they simply do not speak our musical language; when we sing them we have a feeling similar to that which we have when translating from a foreign language. Unless one is an accomplished linguist, one's thoughts do not flow as easily when he is translating as when he is using his native tongue. Again, if we are seeking reasons to explain why we have not been able to make satisfactory use of many of the chorales we have tried to use, another may be that we insist on singing them in parts, that is, in four-part harmony. It has always been the custom, except with us, to have the congregation sing them in unison, the parts other than that of the melody being supplied by the organ. (In the early days they were supplied by the choir.) It has also been usual to precede their singing with a prelude and to have short interludes interpolated between each two lines of the text. Of course, this makes for slowness, for some tediousness in their singing, and for breaking into the train of thought; but the Germans seem not to mind that. We do mind it and have not been able to adapt ourselves to the German manner.

Just an additional word to clarify this stand on the

matter of the chorale. While recognizing the dignity of German church music and the fine conception of the German service as a whole, we may not profitably transplant wholesale their chorales into our situation, for the very good reason that they grew out of situations peculiar to the German people. They are founded upon sentiments which are their own and which grew out of their own natures, their own experiences, and their own needs. We should take over, and have taken over, those which are meaningful to us. And, with profit, we might well continue our study of that which would be most suitable for us and use it. The same thing might be said of the worship music of other Christian peoples; the Scandinavians, for instance, have a literature with which we in America might well be more familiar. But more is necessary than that a tune has been harmonized by Bach to make it suitable for our use.

Luther stands first among the hymn writers of the early Reformation period—some thirty-seven hymns may with confidence be accredited to him—but most of his offerings were revisions, translations, and expansions of earlier material. A few of them are still in use in English-speaking countries, and most of them are—or were—favorites in Germany. The only one that has come into even fairly general use is the great *Ein' feste Burg*, "A mighty fortress is our God." A great historic hymn with an equally great melody, it has been used by many composers. Bach's magnificent cantata based upon it was written for the Reformation Festival of either 1730 or 1739, the first being the celebration of the Reformation movement itself and the second being the Jubilee of the two-hundredth anniversary of the adoption in Saxony of the Evangelical doctrines. Mendelssohn used it for the Finale of his *Reformation Symphony*, Nicolai for his *Fest-Ouvertüre*, Wagner for his *Kaisermarsch*, and Meyerbeer in his grandest of grand operas, *Les Huguenots*. As in the case of the tune "Old Hundredth," attempts have been made to prove that this melody was built up from various portions of the Roman *Gradual*. And such may have been the case, for Luther had been a monk and must have been familar with the *Gradual* tunes and sung them often. Even so, it is a very fine tune which he produced.

This hymn should never be sung at any small public gathering; the midweek prayer meeting attended by only a few of the faithful and usually held in some small room is no place to try to make it effective. It is a grand conception and demands grand conditions both as to numbers of persons and as to space. It expresses the best side of the heroic period of the German Reformation. (No. 67.)

The period from about 1575 through the Thirty Years' War (1618-48) was one of transition in German hymnody. At first the hymns tended toward objectiveness—were "churchly." However, the terrible experiences of the long war brought in an element of subjectiveness—quite a plaintive note similar to that which characterizes much of that which came later. The only true chorale (hymn and tune) which has become anything like a popular favorite in English-speaking countries, according to C. S. Phillips[2] is a product of the period, namely, Martin Rinkart's *Nun danket alle Gott*—"Now thank we all our God"—called the German *Te Deum*. There seems to be no basis in fact for the many stories told of circumstances surrounding its composition; it is simply a hymn of general thanksgiving. (No. 7.)

It is interesting for us to note that the familiar hymn "Lift up your heads, ye mighty gates" (No. 126), Catherine Winkworth's translation from George Weissel, comes from this period also. Although included with the hymns for Palm Sunday, it is really a hymn for Advent, as a careful reading of its text will show.

The Thirty Years' War, which "caused men to look away from this world," doubtless influenced the writing of Paul Gerhardt (1607-76), prince of German hymnodists; for he lived through all of it, being but a boy of eleven years when it began. He was the leading figure of the period from the close of the great war to the beginnings of the Pietist movement, from 1648 to 1680. This was a continuation of the transition period, at least, if not a new one; there was a further departure from the churchly and confessional toward the emotional and devotional. The Rev. W. H. Frere says that "religion in him went deeper than the level of individualistic piety," that it "fertilized a naturally mystic mind," so that his appeal was universal throughout Christendom—it was not limited alone to Lutherans. His influence, therefore, was greater than that of any of his predecessors; he was an inspiration to other hymn writers, among whom were both John and Charles Wesley.

Of the three hymns of Gerhardt in general use, one of which (No. 141, already mentioned) is a rendering of a medieval Latin one, perhaps the most popular is the exquisite Nativity hymn, "All my heart this night rejoices" (No. 91), part of a translation of *Fröhlich soll mein Herze springen*, a poem of fifteen stanzas which Lauxman has called "a glorious series of Christmas thoughts, laid as a garland on the manger at Bethlehem." The singing of stan-

zas 13 and 14 of this hymn is said to have made clear to
Carl H. von Gogatzky—author of the great missionary hymn
beginning,

> Wake Israel from his sleep, O Lord,
> And spread the conquest of Thy Word!

—the meaning of the doctrine of justification by faith. The
stanzas referred to are:

> Guilt no longer can distress me,
>   Son of God, Thou my load
> Bearest to release me.
>   Stain in me Thou findest never;
> I am clean, All my sin
>   Is removed forever.
>
> I am pure, in Thee believing,
>   From Thy store Evermore
> Righteous robes receiving.
>   In my heart I will enfold Thee,
> Treasure rare, Let me there,
>   Loving, ever hold Thee.

The third one by Gerhardt is John Wesley's translation of
O Jesu Christ, mein schönstes Licht—"Jesus, Thy boundless love to me" (No. 222)—which, gratifyingly, seems to
be now taking an added lease on its life. The translation
appeared so early as 1739 in Hymns and Sacred Poems, the
first collection bearing the names of John and Charles Wesley on its title page. In his Plain Account of Christian Perfection John Wesley says that, as he was returning from
Georgia in 1738, "the cry of my heart was,

> O grant that nothing in my soul
> May dwell, but thy pure love alone!

128

O may thy love possess me whole,
  My joy, my treasure, and my crown!
Strange fires far from my heart remove;
  My every act, word, thought, be love!"

This was the second stanza of the original.

Joachim Neander (1650-80), while belonging to the German Reformed school, deserves mention with the Evangelicals of this period if for no other reason than because of his having written what the late Canon Percy Dearmer has said to be the finest song of praise there is, taking into consideration the tune to which it is sung, "Praise to the Lord, the Almighty, the King of Creation!" to *Lobe den Herren.*" Wedded since 1680, this hymn and tune has come into great favor in recent years, since its inclusion in our latest hymnals; it is now one of the most widely sung praise hymns of the Christian Church. (No. 60.)

Tobais Clausnitzer (1619-84), contemporary of Gerhardt, has given us, through Catherine Winkworth's translation, what might well be one of our most helpful hymns were it used, "Blessed Jesus, at Thy word." The tune, *"Liebster Jesu, wir sind hier,"* has been associated with this text since 1671. (No. 310.)

As representative of the Pietists, that group within the Lutheran group which tried to arouse the Evangelical Church from its fossilizing controversy and the effects of the Thirty Years' War, Johann Jacob Schütz (1640-90) and Benjamin Schmolck (1672-1737) should be mentioned. The former, a friend of P. J. Spener, originator of the *Collegia Pietatis,* or prayer meetings, which were responsible for the Pietistic movement and with which he had much to do, Schütz has given us a fine thanksgiving hymn, one which has played a large part in the religious life of Germany. (No. 355.) The other, Benjamin Schmolck, is known to all Christians through his "My Jesus, as Thou wilt!" Something of real interest might be said, if space allowed, of the excellent tune to which this hymn is sung. In fact, there is enough of interest—factual, anecdotal, and otherwise—about the tunes in our hymnals to warrant the writing of another book at least as extensive as this.

Most of the Pietists remained within their Mother Church, but a section broke away and organized themselves into a separate body called the Moravians. This is no place, nor does this writer have either the requisite knowledge or the desire, to discuss the vicissitudes of the *Unitas Fratrum*, or United Brethren, before the old Moravian group found refuge at Herrnhut and their feeble organization was given new life and impetus by Count Zinzendorf. While the vast majority of the hymns by their German writers have been deemed unfit for general use because of their extreme use of the terms of human affection and endearment, yet it was given to John Wesley, says Dean Furneaux, to "reveal to Englishmen the rich treasures of German hymnody." This came about as a result of his association with the Moravians; he had been impressed by the comfort they found through hymn singing during a violent storm while on his way to Georgia in 1736; he knew Count Zinzendorf, was intimate with Peter Böhler, and "was thunderstruck" at the narrations of some Moravian converts. He studied their hymns assiduously, and in a sermon delivered only two years before his death ("On Knowing Christ After the Flesh," 1789) he said: "I translated many of their hymns, for the use of our own congregations. Indeed, as I durst not implicitly follow any man, I did not take all that lay before me; but selected those which I judged to be most scriptural, and most suittable to sound experience." Wesley had an antipathy toward the use of "fondling" terms; especially did he object to the word "dear." It will be remembered that "Jesus, Lover of my soul," although written by Charles Wesley in 1737 and published in the Wesley brothers' *Hymns and Sacred Poems* of 1740, did not appear in any other of their collections until six years after the death of John, doubtless because of his objection to the word "Lover." In many of the hymnals of the period the word "Refuge" was substituted for it. Wesley was careful, in his sermon, to continue: "Yet I am not sure that I have taken sufficient care to pare off every improper word or expression."

Two translations by John Wesley from the more than two thousand hymns written by Count Zinzendorf are "Jesus, Thy blood and righteousness" (No. 205) and "O Thou, to whose all-searching sight" (No. 360). Another of Zinzendorf's hymns, and one of his best, is "Jesus, still lead on," which has an excellent tune written by another Pietist writer, Adam Drese, who is known to our hymnals, however, only as a musician. (No. 336.)

Although the number of writers of German hymns is great, but one more need be mentioned, namely, Gerhard Tersteegen (1697-1769), a pure mystic who, while founding no sect of his own, held aloof from Lutheranism; he was not interested in organized religion. He, also, greatly influenced John Wesley, who gave us his great hymn, "Thou hidden Love of God" (No. 375), which perhaps was suggested by the well-known lines opening St. Augustine's *Confessions*: "Thou movest us to delight in praising Thee;

for Thou hast formed us for Thyself, and our hearts are restless till they find rest in Thee."

Before Tersteegen's death the era of Enlightenment had begun in Europe; religious thinking became cold, theistic rather than Christian in the attempts made to rationalize it. Hymns became odes and lyrics; of the few which have come over to us the best-known ones are "We plow the fields and scatter" (No. 544), by Matthias Claudius (1740-1815), and "O happy home, where Thou art loved the dearest" (No. 427), by Carl J. P. Spitta (1801-59), perhaps our finest hymn of the home.

Some fine tunes, however, come to us from this period, among them being "Austrian Hymn," by F. J. Haydn; "Lyons," by his brother, Johann Michael; and "St. Hilda," by Justin H. Knecht. Aside from these and, perhaps, a very few others, the debt to our hymnals to the later Germans is negligible.

The terms psalm-singing and Calvinism are, in the minds of many people, synonymous. To an extent this is true, yet we should remember that while all Calvinists have been psalm singers not all psalm singers have been Calvinists. The Psalms have always been the property of all branches of the Church, and all branches of the Church sing psalms either in their metrified form or in the form of hymns based on portions from the Book of Psalms.

Calvin, returning to Geneva after his first visit there, urged by Farel to do so, was confronted and challenged with the problem of providing some way in which Reformers might worship. They had no forms through which they might express their Christian devotion, everything with which they had been familiar having been discarded. There was no incense used, no holy oil; there were no candles; there was no chanting or intoning, no altar; there were no vestments—only black robes. They used only bread and wine, which had no significance other than that they were symbolic, at the Eucharist.

Perhaps Calvin's most remarkable contribution was that of providing a form of worship, for he was little more than a layman where Luther had been a monk and Zwingli and Knox had been priests. While the Reformed Church held in common with other reformed bodies the use of the vernacular in worship, and, as the Lutheran, made prominent the sermon, it broke completely with historic ritual; it was a new plant which was destined to have a remarkable growth and influence.

Many people do not like John Calvin, yet many will agree with E. Stanton Hodgin, a Unitarian minister in Los Angeles, who said he could count on the fingers of one hand all the men who had lived in the last six centuries who could "be as illy spared as could John Calvin." The Mother Church which had "held mankind true" during the dark ages had "lost its vision" in the fifteenth century and had become an end in itself, living off the credulity of the people. Savonarola, Wycliffe, Huss, and others had cried out in vain against it. Then Luther revolted. But, with the coming of the Peasants' War in Germany, the political rather than the moral element rose to prominence; and Lutheranism, while holding its course, became disheartened, uncertain of its mission and even of itself.

With the death of Zwingli, the brilliant beginning of the reform movement in Switzerland had largely played itself out and was not quite sure where it was going. Then, when the whole enterprise seemed on the verge of failure, came John Calvin, under whom the Reformation found itself, gained strength, and for the next two centuries influenced every movement "in the direction of the realization of truth and freedom," no matter where it started—Switzerland, France, Germany, the Low Countries, Scotland, England, and America. For nearly two centuries the greatest leaders —those who were the most heroic morally, spiritually, physically—were, for the greater part, Calvinists.

Calvin was not a pioneer of reform—he belonged to the second generation of reformers. Where the pioneers had cleared the fields he cultivated them; where they had sown the first seeds he cared for them and gathered the harvest. Luther had influenced more than half of Germany; Zwingli, much of German Switzerland; Farel, Geneva (not then a part of Switzerland) and most of France; and the sentiment for reform was strong in Scotland, England, and in all parts of Europe.

A Frenchman, a lawyer as well as a preacher (he never became a priest), who reached intellectual maturity and his final convictions by the time he was twenty-five; who thought clearly, had a genius for organization and demonstration, and loved orderliness; who was naturally timid and retiring, never robust; who was quite the opposite in personality to Luther—Calvin was one of the most convincing men who ever lived. He was remarkably stimulating to his preachers, giving to each entire responsibility for his service, for the "Genevan Liturgy" can scarcely be called a liturgy, properly differing as it does so much from the established ones. It was simple, primitive, calling for each minister to decide what passages from the Scriptures he should read, what he should preach, as well as what the people might sing. The preacher needed no robes, no altar; not even a church building was an absolute necessity. The singing of the people provided the emotional element theretofore supplied by features of the rituals of other and older churches. Their belief in the universal priesthood of believers made this feature of their worship stand out prominently, and therein lay much of its strength. Is it any wonder singing played the part that it did? Where its tendency was to reduce all—the great and the small, the learned and the unlearned, prince and pauper—to a common kinship? When it gave opportunity to all to express their prayer and praise directly to the Almighty?

Luther, great lover of music as we have seen, was not averse to the use of secular melodies with his hymns; in fact, he welcomed them. Calvin, no great lover of music, had no use for the frivolous French tunes of his day. Luther found no reason to object to hymns of free, human composition; in fact, he sought for poets to provide them. Calvin would have nothing in his service for which he could not claim scriptural authority; he found there his authority for congregational singing and felt the advantage of texts written in metrical forms. If he were to use only church song based on Holy Writ and if it were to have general appeal, he saw no way out but to provide metrical renderings of portions of the Bible.

Practically, this meant that only the Psalms could be used. He did not forbid the use of other biblical material (there was some of it in all of the early psalters)—it just did not lend itself so well to his immediate purpose. And because of Calvin's having sanctioned the use of metrical psalms for worship purposes at Geneva, so great was the influence of that sanction, it followed wherever the Calvinistic doctrine flourished.

Let us again be reminded that Calvin was not a pioneer. Metrical psalms, many of them, had been written before Clément Marot began writing them and before Calvin took Marot under his wing. Margaret, Queen of Navarre, in marked contrast to her *Heptaméron,* had rendered some psalms into meter, and through them, perhaps, had shown Marot that possibilities lay in that direction. The German book of 1524 by Luther and Walther contained versified versions of some psalms (*Ein' feste Burg* is Luther's own rendering of the Forty-sixth); and in England, Miles Coverdale published about 1539, the year of Calvin's Strassburg book, his *Goostly Psalms and Spiritualle Songes,* which had these lines of dedication on its title page:

> Be not ashamed, I warrande thee
> Though thou be rude in song and ryme,
> Thou shalt to youth some occasion be
> In godly sports to passe theyr tyme.

How was it, then, that the metrical psalms of the type approved by Calvin have been the ones so greatly to influence England and America? Doubtless because of the profound impression Calvinism made on the numerous refugees from England, who fleeing the intolerable conditions which obtained under Queen Mary, first went to Frankfort and then on to Geneva. They had taken with them books containing some of the pharaphrases of Thomas Sternhold, who had been an official, before the persecutions, at the court of Henry VIII and Edward VI.

CHORALES AND METRICAL PSALMS

The story of the evolution of the Anglo-Genevan and English psalters is too involved to admit of discussion here; enough to say that when the exiles returned to England they were thoroughly impregnated with the psalmody of Calvinism. This fact, together with the impress made upon Scotland by John Knox upon his return from Geneva, so thoroughly "sold" those two countries on the idea of using only metrical psalms for congregational use that for nearly two centuries nothing else was heard in the free churches.

While there is almost no textual material from the early psalters in use today, we do have some of our most excellent tunes from them. Reference will be made to them in the next chapter, where there will also be further discussion of the metrical paraphrases of the psalms, because their relation to early hymns in English was very close.

There is, however, one tune current today which comes from the 1551 *Genevan Psalter* and a rhymed psalm from the *Psalter* published in London by John Daye in 1560-61 and in the *Anglo-Genevan Psalter* of 1561; namely, the tune, "Old Hundredth," anonymous, although quite generally accredited to Louis Bourgeois, who was Calvin's dependable musician and the editor of the *Psalter* when it first appeared, and the 100th Psalm, paraphrased by William Kethe into "All people that on earth do dwell" (No. 13).

IX

ENGLAND'S DEVELOPMENT OF THE HYMN

SPECULATION IS AN INTERESTING, THOUGH SELDOM A PROFIT-able, undertaking. One finds interest and a certain satisfaction in theorizing as to what might have been the result had the Marian refugees gravitated toward Wittenberg rather than toward Geneva. What might have been the course of the development of the *Book of Common Prayer* had Henry VIII not suppressed Miles Coverdale's *Goostly Psalms and Spiritualle Songes*? Might not the whole history of the English Church have been changed? And, as the general trend of events in England has been greatly influenced by the Church, one might ponder on what might have been had the English and the Scottish peoples seen fit to follow Luther instead of Calvin.

But these peoples chose to follow Calvin; and as a result the development of hymnody, as such, was greatly retarded by the influence and example of Geneva. No native English congregational hymnody worthy of the name was produced until well into the eighteenth century, even though England had produced a Chaucer, a Spenser, a Shakespeare, and a Milton. There was no lack of appreciation of the value and effectiveness of congregational song, however, as is amply attested by the writers of the period. George Herbert and a few others wrote moralizations, allegories, soliloquies, and meditations in verse; but they were intended for use in pri vate, not public devotions. In the Preface to Simon Browne's *Hymns and Spiritual Songs*, 1720, we are told that, to the time of Watts, the only hymns in common use "either in private families or in Christian assemblies" were those of William Barton, John Mason, and Thomas Shepherd, together with "an attempt to turn some of George Herbert's poems into common metre," and some sacramental hymns by now-forgotten authors.

But little more need be said than has already been said about the metrical psalm, for our concern is more with hymnody than with psalmody. Yet our present-day hymnals are enriched through having retained a number of the older metrified psalms, especially those from the *Scottish Psalter* of 1650 and from the *New Version* of Tate and Brady. Let it again be said: any attempt to discuss adequately the development of this branch of church song within the scope of this book would be quite out of the question. It might, however, be profitable to present as briefly as possible some of the signal elements of such development.

Various editions of the French- and Anglo-Genevan Psalters appeared during the years from 1539 to 1562 and, in a number of instances, continued in use for quite some time longer. The *English Psalter*, a reproduction of the Anglo-Genevan, appeared in 1560; and the edition of this book which appeared but one year later marked the first real difference between the later psalmody of the English and Scottish churches. The 1562 edition, known as "Sternhold and Hopkins," or the *Old Version*, was a real achievement and held its place for more than a century. Owing to an obstinate insistence upon as exact a rendering from the Hebrew as was possible, its versification was crude even for its day. The difficulties of translation are always great; in the case of the Psalms, with but few exceptions, they are well-nigh insuperable. Yet, as time went on, noticeable improvement was made, as even a casual comparison of the *Old Version* with the *New Version* of Tate and Brady, which first appeared in 1696, will show. From the *Old Version* we have no texts in our modern books; but we have retained some of its best tunes, namely, those with the prefix "Old": "Old 100th"; "Old 113th," the tune to which John Wesley sang "I'll praise my Maker while I've breath" (No. 513); and "Old 134th," or "St. Michael."

The renderings of the psalms as they appeared in the *New Version* give the impression of being quite hymnlike; they show a distinct advance. Less hymnlike, because of the Puritan insistence upon literalness, were the translations of Francis Rous in his version, long and familiarly known as the *Scottish Psalter of 1650*. Some of these renderings by Rous have a quaint beauty which has greatly endeared them to our worshiping people. Especially worthy of notice are the versions of Psalm 23 (No. 70) and the first part of Psalm 84 (No. 383). Their fidelity in translation to the King James rendering is amazing. Of all the metrified versions of the Twenty-third Psalm—and there are many of them—this has, perhaps best stood the test of time. Sung to "Martyrdom," that sturdy old tune from the country of the Covenanters, it become one of the great worship songs of all time—an expression of devotion and gratitude which has not been surpassed. (No. 70.)

The difficulties of translation, especially in the case of the Psalms, has been mentioned; yet the Psalms, as is true of much else in the Scriptures, are filled with suggestive material for hymnographers. It is by adaptation and assimilation, however, rather than by direct translation, that they best serve their purpose of providing suitable worship material; some of our greatest hymns are the result of hymn writers' having recognized this. To illustrate how this works out, let us compare Sir Henry Williams Baker's "The King of love my Shepherd is" (No. 353) with the Rous version of Psalm 23. There may be some question as to preference, but the comparison is interesting in so far as it shows how the treatment of a common subject may be varied. "The King of love my Shepherd is" is undoubtedly one of the best renderings of this psalm in the English language. While this lyric is a reflection of the content and spirit of the psalm, it is more than that: it is an expression of other references in the Scriptures to the Lord as the Shepherd of His people. The third stanza is suggested, of course, by the words of the parable of the lost sheep, "When he hath found it, he layeth it on his shoulders, rejoicing." (Luke 15:5.)

Where else in all literature do we find such an absence of all doubt, misgiving, fear, anxiety as in this psalm? It breathes to the utmost the quiet confidence of the believer.

In all editions of the early psalters there were included, as an appended group, certain hymns and metrical pharaphrases of scriptural passages and material from prayer books. This, however, comprised but a small part of the psalters, and one must make his own inferences as to their real significance; there was doubtless no intent that they should be used in public worship services.

Since the earliest significant writer of hymns belonging to the pre-Watts era, George Wither, has no representation in our hymnals, but little time will be devoted to mention of his writings. While it was first given to George Wither to realize the requisites of a good hymn, he should not be compared with such men as Bishop Ken, George Herbert, or Isaac Watts; for he was in no sense their equal. Yet he should receive full credit for his contribution which, as he expressed it, was to illustrate "the particular mysteries of the Christian faith." This era is represented, however, by selections from Bishop Ken and George Herbert.

From Bishop Ken, Chaplain of the English Court of Charles II, Chaplain of the English Fleet at Tangiers, where Moorish pirates were carrying on their depredations, who refused the use of his house by Nell Gwyn (and was made bishop as a result); who, with other ministers (John Wesley's father among them), refused to follow James II's order to proclaim from their pulpits his "Declaration of Indulgence"; who had the famous tilt with Judge Jeffries; who refused to swear allegiance to James II's successor and, tired of the conflict with Britain's rulers, retired from active service; than whom the English Church has produced no greater man—fearless, faithful, gentle, kindly—we have two really great hymns: "Awake, my soul, and with the sun" (No. 34) and "All praise to Thee, my God, this night" (No. 51). It is from these hymns —and from his "Midnight Hymn" also—that we get our Long Meter Doxology, "Praise God, from whom all blessings flow."

George Herbert, who borrowed the ancient idea of the philosophers's stone, which, could it be found, would transmute all baser materials into gold, and who applied the idea to his *The Elixer*; whose writings were highly favored by Susannah Wesley; whose memory has been kept alive by Methodists; great lover of music and friend of Izaak Walton has given us "Teach me, my God and King" (No. 320) from *The Elixer*, and "Let all the world in every corner sing" (No. 8), entitled "Antiphon" in his *The Temple*, from which No. 320 is also taken.

So much has been written about Isaac Watts and his great contribution that but little time need be devoted to him, not because of any desire or intent to belittle or ignore him, but because there is an extensive literature dealing with him and his work which is available to any and all who may be interested. This, however, should be said of him: while he was not "the inventor of the English hymn," he did establish its right to a place in modern Christian worship—his hymns were epoch-making. And they grew directly out of his attempts to accommodate the content of metrical psalmody to Christian truth—to "make David speak like a Christian." When Watts and other poets of the time realized the difference between lines written for private meditation and devotion and those written for corporate public praise, England was well on her way toward making her great contribution to Christian hymnody.

To Isaac Watts must go the greatest credit for this. He succeeded where others failed; he excelled all who preceded him and the most of those who followed him; he succeeded in convincing Christians generally that the hymn was a normal and legitimate vehicle for the expression of corporate praise. The two main streams of church song, paraphrases of Scripture and devotional lyric poetry, came together in his offerings. Most of Watts's metrical renderings of the Psalms, it is true, have now disappeared from our hymnals; but there are a few which we still retain and which, doubtless, we shall retain for a long time to come. Among them are the first and fourth stanzas of No. 17, "From all that dwell below the skies," his paraphrase of the shortest psalm, the 117th; No. 82, his imitation" of a part of Psalm 36; No. 89, "Joy to the World!" a free rendering of the last part of Psalm 98; No. 479, "Jesus shall reign where'er the sun," the "greatest of all missionary hymns," Psalm 72; No. 513, already mentioned; and, greatest of all, No. 533, "O God, our help in ages past," more of a hymn than a metrical psalm.

Joseph Addison, whose five hymns appeared in *The Spectator* some five years after Watts issued his *Hymns and Spiritual Songs,* 1707, was too much of an individualist to be called a follower or an imitator of the latter, although he may have had suggested to him the thought of writing some hymns through reading those of Watts. He deserves mention because two of his five hymns have established for themselves a definite place in modern hymnals. They are "The spacious firmament on high" (No. 66) and "When all Thy mercies, O my God" (No. 542), the first an excellent commentary of Psalm 19, written for the purpose of "strengthening and confirming faith in the mind of man," and the second a beautiful and touching expression of praise, gratitude, and thanksgiving. So meticulous that he was known to have stopped the presses of *The Spectator* in order to make such minor corrections as the altering of a preposition or a conjunction, Addison's style was long deemed the model for English prose.

As in the case of Isaac Watts and for much the same reasons, little need be said about John and Charles Wesley, the former one of the ablest translators of hymns and the latter quite generally acclaimed the greatest hymn writer of all time.

England presented a sorry picture at the beginning of th

eighteenth century. "In Walpole's day the English clergy were the idlest and most lifeless in the world—the most remiss in their labours, and the least severe in their lives." With very few exceptions the bishops spent their time in gay living in London, utterly neglecting their dioceses; Montesquieu wrote, "In the higher circles everyone laughs if one talks religion"; drunkenness and foul talk characterized all men of fashion; leaders in England had no belief in goodness; there was political stagnation. Because of the rise of manufacturing, the population of the cities greatly increased; no new parishes had been formed in many years; there were no schools other than those which had been founded by Edward VI and Elizabeth; drink shops advertised, "Get drunk for a penny and dead drunk for two pennies." The Blue Laws of Puritan Connecticut cannot be compared in point of severity and cruelty to those of the period in England: men were hung for trivial offenses—twenty young men were found hanging in front of Newgate on one single morning.

Yet, as always, there were at least a few good people, the Wesleys being among them. It was such a world in which John and Charles Wesley found themselves when they left the clear, clean atmosphere of Epworth. The very conditions which confronted them were a challenge; and they met that challenge by instituting a revival of religion which, it has been repeatedly said, saved England's soul.

John Wesley's "burning conviction" of the tremendous possibilities which lay in the people's part in the worship of God and in the efficacy of hymn singing in that worship, his belief in the utilization of hymns for "raising the devotion" and for instructing and fixing the faith of his followers, was in large part responsible for the extraordinary impetus given hymn singing in England.

Charles Wesley, man of great charm, of dauntless courage and integrity, intelligent, magnanimous, with extraordinary powers of expression, who provided a song for every occasion yet of whom his brother said, "His least praise was his talent for poetry," and of whom none other than John Julian said, "Taking quantity and quality into consideration" he was, perhaps, "the great hymn-writer of all ages"—such a man needs nothing further said in his honor. No greater respect can be paid him than to rest his case on the judgment of others; his hymns are known to all of us and have been sung by us since childhood.

Perhaps Charles Wesley's greatest contribution, other than that which has to do with the content of his hymns, lay in his emancipation of English hymnody from the shackles of form which had been laid upon it by his predecessors. He refused to be limited to the confines of long, short, common, and the popular ballad meters. His genius demanded a freedom of expression which is not discernible in other and earlier hymnists. Further his musical taste and feeling was not satisfied by the accepted "proper" and "common" tunes. He wrote in at least twenty different meters and was master of them all; perhaps no other poet has felt equally at home in their varied use, nor has any other presented such a challenge to writers of hymn tunes.

The recognized composers of his day who were at all interested in writing for the Church were writing for the Established Church—there were none of much standing in the musical world who were interested in furnishing music for the independents. The situation resulting from Charles Wesley's unremitting flow of devotional lyrics called for a comparable fund of tunes. Those hymns which he wrote in the established meters were, of course, supplied with the fine old psalm tunes; but the "peculiar meters" demanded something new. John Wesley, who believed the devil should not have all of the good tunes, sought and took tunes from every available source. He encouraged unknown amateurs and as a result the Wesleyan Revival loosed a flood of new hymn tunes, some of which were a real and lasting contribution. Not all of the "old Methodist tunes" were musical doggerel, no matter what standard may be used in judging them. They were tunes which had a popular appeal—tuneful melodies, folk songs, and others—many being new and especially composed for the Wesley hymns. In short, anything was used which might prove suitable for the single purpose the Wesley brothers had in mind: to make Christians out of non-Christians.

The Wesleys not only added greatly to the store of hymns then available and correspondingly enriched it; they established new types (by way of emphasizing the evangelistic note and the hymn of experience), provided the basis for a churchly or liturgical hymnody, and made valid the criterion that a hymn should be a poem.

It is interesting to note that for nearly one-hundred years English hymnody had its only real development in non-Conformist circles. It is true that Charles Wesley never left the English Church; but it is likewise true that the English Church has never shown anything like cordiality to any of his offerings, with the possible exception of "Hark! the herald angels sing." In the light of the effect upon England of the Wesleyan Revival with its emphasis on hymn singing, a feeling amounting almost to amazement comes over us when we realize that more than sixty years after Charles Wesley's death John Mason Neale could innocently ask the name of the author of "Hark! the herald angels sing"! The answer, of course, is that editors of hymnals other than Wesleyan failed to give him credit for his work.

Many were the followers and imitators of Watts and Wesley, but few of them contributed anything essentially new. More than fifty well-known English hymn writers of the last half of the eighteenth and the first half of the nineteenth centuries might be mentioned, and with profit; but there would be nothing gained by doing so here and now. The majority of them are represented in present-day hymnals by not more than one hymn each, although there are marked exceptions, and it is but fair to say that some of the single offerings of these writers are among the finest hymns we have. It is enough to say, further, that, until Reginald Heber appeared, most of them were independents. Heber marked a new development, when the greater number of hymns seemed to emanate from the Church of England, chiefly from its clergy. Horatius Bonar, of whom we have no memoir, was the outstanding exception. With the help of Henry Hart Milman, author of the fine Palm Sunday hymn "Ride on! ride on in majesty!" (No. 125), Bishop Heber was one of the first to arrange hymns in order for the Christian Year and to encourage their free use by the Church of England.

As the nineteenth century advanced, women writers, following the lead of Anne Steele, increased in numbers, contributing new elements of tenderness, sweetness, and insight

From the middle of the nineteenth century the Oxford movement, nothing less than a High-Church revival, gave a tremendous impetus to hymn production. The whole matter of the type of hymn to be used in the English Church becoming a major issue in the controversy, the search for hymnic material compatible with the thinking of the leaders of the movement led to a revival of interest in the old Latin liturgical hymns, many of which were translated and suggested for use in that Church. The popularity of the evangelical type of hymn was such that it began forcing its way into English Church use, and the alarm which this caused its leaders drove them to seek an acceptable antidote—a hymn which was primarily liturgical.

The difference between the evangelical hymn and that which is liturgical is that the former is the personal expression of the individual believer as over against the expression of the Church; it is an expression of individual inward experience versus that of common, or corporate, experience. There is a freedom of use found in the evangelical hymn which is quite a contrast with the restrictions of the liturgical: whereas the former may be used freely at any time and place where its use might be advantageous, the other, strictly speaking, may be used only at such time and in such way as may be specified in the Calendar.

Naturally, this revived interest in hymns in High-Church circles called for books which might serve the Church. Within a few years some one hundred and fifty were produced; not all, however, were collections of hymns, that is, poems to be sung. Several of them were books of devotional verse—some the work of individuals, others compilations. The great interest manifested in translating the medieval and later Latin hymns into a singable English acted as a stimulus to scholars in other language fields, notably German, resulting in a renewed interest in the hymns of Germany, almost none

of which had come to light since John Wesley. Here the best
work was done by scholarly women, among them being
Frances E. Cox, who gave use "Sing praise to God who
reigns above" (No. 355); Jane L. Borthwick and her sister,
Sarah Findlater, translators of such excellent hymns as "Be
still, my soul: the Lord is on thy side," which, sung to "Find-
landia," has received such a generous welcome in all of our
churches in recent years (No. 73), "Jesus, still lead on" (No.
336), and the great hymn of the Christian home, "O happy
home, where Thou art loved the dearest" (No. 427); and
Catherine Winkworth, who contributed "Now thank we all
our God" (No. 7), "Praise to the Lord, the Almighty, the
King of creation!" (No. 60), "All my heart this night rejoices" (No. 91), all of which were referred to earlier, and
others which stamp her as having had more to do with popu-
larizing "hymns from the land of Luther" than any other
one person.

Among the men, leaders in the Oxford movement who
have made noteworthy contributions and who are members
of the group of more than fifty referred to, are John Keble,
John Mason Neale, Cardinal Newman, Frederick W. Faber,
and Edward Caswall, the last three of whom left the Anglican
Church for the Roman Catholic.

The famous *Hymns Ancient and Modern* emerged as a
direct consequence of the Tractarian movement, the competition between the numerous hymnbooks which had been
produced preventing the success of any. Sensibly, certain
leaders, recognizing the lack of anything approaching una-
nimity in the Church's use of hymns, succeeded in getting
the publishers and owners of many of the competing books
to withdraw them, and set about compiling a selection which

would be acceptable to the majority of the churches. That the movement was successful may be judged from the fact that 10,340 churches out of 13,639 adopted the new book, a sale of more than sixty million copies being shown from the time it was first issued, in 1861, up to and including the year 1912.

Hymns Ancient and Modern has profoundly affected the hymnody of the entire Church during the years; a great many of our now most favored hymns first appeared in some one of its several editions. Because of their number it is difficult to decide upon those which should be singled out for special mention, but a purely personal choice of ten out of the many would be:

"The King of love my Shepherd is," Sir Henry Williams Baker, No. 353

"As with gladness men of old," W. Chatterton Dix, No. 90

"Onward, Christian soldiers!" Sabine Baring-Gould, No. 280

"O day of rest and gladness," Christopher Wordsworth, No. 396

"The Church's one foundation," Samuel J. Stone, No. 381

"Saviour, again to Thy dear Name we raise," John Ellerton, No. 29

"Lead, kindly Light," John Henry Newman, No. 514

"O Jesus, I have promised," J. E. Bode, No. 226

"Fight the good fight," J. S. B. Monsell, No. 286

"Angel voices, ever singing," Francis Pott, No. 15

This list is, of course, quite an arbitrary one, and doubtless others would make different selections; but the purpose in presenting these is to show how wide and varied is the character of the material in this great hymnal. The effect of *Hymns Ancient and Modern* upon the hymnody of the Church at large has been profound and should be repeatedly emphasized.

One marked reason for its astonishing success was its music, which was fresh and which had a pleasing type of tune. Here John Bacchus Dykes and W. H. Monk became known, as did Sir John Stainer, Sir Joseph Barnby, Sir Arthur Sullivan, and other Victorian hymn-tune writers. A hymnal being a book for singing, always stands or falls on the nature of the tunes it carries. No matter what we may now think of the tunes of the late-nineteenth-century English organists, they satisfied the tune longings of the people of their day and made for the success of this superb book. It was the musical element which made it appeal to the non-Conformist. He objected seriously to its general Anglo-Catholic leaning; but, in keeping with the attitudes of all peoples of all times, he cared little what he sang about if only he liked what he sang it to. Only recently has a healthy reaction to the Dykes-Barnby-Sullivan type of tune set in; but more of that later.

At the beginning of this century a group of men in England, all interested in music even if not all professional musicians, set about renovating the then prevalent hymnody of that country. Among them were Percy Dearmer, Athelstan Riley, Ralph Vaughan Williams, Nicholas Gatty, and Gustav von Holst, all competent, well known, and highly respected. They produced *The English Hymnal* and submitted it as "a humble companion to the Book of Common Prayer for use in the Church." "In Christian song," they said, "churches have forgotten their quarrels and men have lost their limitations, because they have reached the high ground where the soul is content to affirm and to adore. The hymns of Christendom show more clearly than anything else that there is even now such a thing as the unity of the Spirit." Here is a clear sounding of that ecumenical note which has continued to be sounded through hymnic offerings ever since, becoming louder and more insistent in those of the last few years.

The prime consideration in choosing music for *The English Hymnal* was that it be congregational in character; that its melody rather than its harmony stand out; that familiar melodies be provided in so far as feasible, although care was exercised to exclude "old favorites" on the basis that there was no particular merit in their being merely "old" or in the fact that they were once "favorites." The editors' standards were kept high; they demonstrated through their selection that a tune may be respectable musically and at the same time be melodious and singable. "A tune has no more right to be dull than it has to be demoralizing," they said. While its text was less a departure from the conventional than its music, *The English Hymnal* nevertheless aroused anew the always-present interest in hymnbook making; and this book was soon succeeded by others following the same general lines as to content but with this distinct difference: they were not offered for the use of the English Church. *The Fellowship Hymn Book, The Oxford Hymnal, Songs of Praise, Hymns of the Kingdom,* came along; such men as Martin Shaw and F. J. Gillman joined the ranks of those mentioned previously; and the Church world awoke to the astonishing fact that the matter of hymnbook making in England had been, in large measure, taken from the hands of the clergy by able, sincere, Christian musicians.

England's contribution has been great; it is quite impossible adequately to evaluate it. Always a singing people the English have seen and participated in the evolution of English hymnody from the early Catholic days when all that was available for use was the Latin hymns. They sang the metrified psalms; they read the early devotional poetry and sang such parts of it as could be made singable; they assisted in developing, and tolerated much of, the variety of "psalms, hymns, and spiritual songs" which came along with the many movements connected with the birth and growth of the independent churches; they sang with enthusiasm the hymns of Watts, Wesley, and others; they became aware of the real awakening of their State Church; they purchased millions of copies of *Hymns Ancient and Modern* and other later books; and they are following with enthusiasm the later offerings of their musician-hymnists. Their contribution to American hymnody is greater than can be sufficiently acknowledged. George Herbert early sounded the note which all England has since been repeating (No. 8):

> Let all the world in every corner sing:
>   My God and King!
> The heavens are not too high,
> His praise may thither fly;
> The earth is not too low,
> His praises there may grow.
> Let all the world in every corner sing:
>   My God and King!
>
> Let all the world in every corner sing:
>   My God and King!
> The Church with psalms must shout,
> No door can keep them out:
> But, more than all, the heart
> Must bear the longest part.
> Let all the world in every corner sing:
>   My God and King!

X

OUR AMERICAN HERITAGE AND CONTRIBUTION

GEORGE A. GORDON ONCE WROTE A VOLUME ENTITLED *My Education and Religion,* in which he said he had long wanted to write another book on the subject "From Authority Through Anarchy to Insight." Inasmuch as he never got around to writing the second book, it may be legitimate to borrow its suggestive title as the general thesis for this discussion. It vividly suggests the stages through which our American hymnody has passed, especially so if we take the three key words to mean:

Authority: that power derived from opinion, respect, esteem, or long-established reputation, such as the *authority* of primacy, example, or prestige.

Anarchy: confusion or disorder in general; the assertion of individual liberty; license; an absence of regulatory powers.

Insight: intellectual discernment; understanding; penetration; the power of seeing into a situation; a reflective knowing.

Certainly, in its beginnings our sacred song had the authority derived from opinion and long-established reputation: that authority gained from its use in other countries by our forefathers. Each of the successive Protestant English-speaking colonies planted in the New World brought along with them the *Old Version* of the Psalms—Sternhold and Hopkins—

except that which landed at Plymouth. This group brought with them that book so gracefully referred to by Longfellow in his *The Courtship of Miles Standish,* where John Alden finds Priscilla:

Open wide on her lap lay the well-worn psalm-book of Ainsworth,
Printed in Amsterdam, the words and the music together,
Rough-hewn, angular notes, like the stones in the wall of a church-
    yard,
Darkened and overhung by the running vine of the verses.

Henry Ainsworth, compiler of this book known as *Ainsworth's Psalter,* was one of the first who underwent religious exile from England, was a noted Hebrew scholar, and became the "teacher" of that congregation in Amsterdam with which those who later became the Pilgrims had "fairly amicable relations" before going on to Leyden in 1609. The book has interest, as has been pointed out by Waldo Selden Pratt, because it contains a prose translation of the Psalms which coincides in point of time almost exactly with that of the King James Version of 1611; because each psalm carries with it a pertinent comment; because, in parallel column, is to be found a metrical translation in varied meters quite at variance with the common "short" form of the older Sternhold and Hopkins; and because there are here some thirty-nine different tunes, three out of four being in the minor mode.

We are not concerned with the text, interesting as it is; for none of Ainsworth's renderings of the psalms have come down to us. The book, made in Holland for the use of temporary residents familiar with the type of song then prevalent in England, shows the influence of the French and Dutch Reformed Churches, a curious blend of styles. Brought to these shores in 1620, it had slight use when compared with the use of the *Old Version,* which came with the Massachusetts Bay group ten years later. It does interest us, however, in that it contained three tunes now quite common to our hymnody— one, of course, being "Old Hundredth"; another, the famous old battle song (the "Huguenot Marseillaise") "Old Hundred and Thirteenth," sung by John Wesley; and the third, "Toulon," favorite of Congregationalists and Presbyterians but not of the Methodists.

Had the American colonists in general taken up this book of Henry Ainsworth with its interesting music and varied metrical renderings of the Psalms, the whole course of American hymnody might have been different. Never in favor with the great majority of the colonists, it was, however, adopted in Salem, where it found use until 1667, and in Plymouth, where the Pilgrims and their descendants used it until 1692, the year after the colony became a part of Massachusetts.

While the Boston colonists, as well as those to the south, brought with them, and used, their copies of the *Old Version* with its commonplace "short" tunes, it was not long before that spirit of independence which prompted them to emigrate to the new country again asserted itself. In this instance the assertion took the form of a demand that a completely new version of the Psalms be provided, this new one to adhere more strictly to the original Hebrew than did any of the others which might have been available. The result was the famous *Bay Psalm Book,* issued in 1640, the first complete book printed in what is now the United States, and which was the only book of its kind used in New England for more than a century. It ran through many editions reaching the twenty-seventh in 1762. It was not until the ninth edition, in 1698, that any tunes were added—and then only about a dozen, of which all but four were in common meter. Only "Old Hundredth" is now in common use.

The low estate into which congregational singing fell during the life of *The Bay Psalm Book* needs no mention here; it has been hashed over *ad nauseam*. Regardless of its causes, and there were many, it became what it did become because of the authority which it derived from opinion and established custom. The resulting "controversie of singing" involved more than the matter of tunes sung; Tate and Brady had issued their *New Version* and *The Scottish Psalter* had been in use in Scotland since about the time *The Bay Psalm Book* first appeared. Incoming settlers brought, along with other effects, their psalters. There must have been a considerable leaning in the direction of their use, for here again was the authority of familiarity. The *New Version* was held in high favor by the more liberally minded until the paraphrases of Watts entered the picture, whereas *The Scottish Psalter*, until well into the latter part of the nineteenth century, held sway among those who were Calvinistically minded. With the coming of the Watts psalms and hymns, authority began to wane; for the spirit of revolt was beginning to make itself manifest.

Early in 1700 Increase Mather issued a book entitled *The Order of the Gospel*, which was followed a few months later by another, *The Gospel Order Revised*, of unknown authorship, the latter a reply to the former, the two books becoming part of a long-drawn-out theological controversy which shook Boston religious circles, led to the establishment of the Brattle Street Church, and further led to "the parting of the ways of the Arminian movement from the ancient Calvinistic Congregationalism of New England." So said Thomas J. Holmes, Mather's bibliographer. In other words, these books represented different sides in the battle between orthodox Congregationalism and Unitarianism, which conflict, naturally, had far-reaching effects upon all later hymnody. Although the liberals were willing to continue to sing Watts with certain limitations—with their fingers crossed, as it were—there developed an insistence that he be "fixed up" somewhat; hymn "tinkerers" got busy and the spirit of anarchy grew apace.

Early Unitarianism was less a protest against Trinitarianism than a reaction against the complacent, conventional dogmatism of the time. Brattle Street Church, in 1753, took a bold stand on the matter of hymn singing, adopting Tate and Brady, but with an appendix containing hymns of their own selection. That their action had influence may be judged from the fact that, toward the close of the century, Unitarian ministers were serving practically all the Congregational churches in and around Boston; for in these churches similar action was taken. The revolt against the sole use of psalms and even of "Watts, entire" grew—it became a matter of reproach for "liberal" churches to use only Watts.

The Presbyterians, a psalm-singing church by inheritance, began having trouble when attempts were made to introduce hymn singing. While George Whitefield favored the use of psalms rather than hymns, the evangelical fervor resulting from the Great Awakening demanded another and quite different expression than that afforded by the psalms alone. Just why Whitefield was not cordial to the Wesleyan hymnody, with which he was undoubtedly familiar, is a matter for speculation. The Great Awakening, however, raised questions concerning the old psalmody which resulted, in 1741, in splitting the Presbyterian body into "Old Side" and "New Side" synods.

Samuel Davies, for a time a missionary in Virginia, later president of what is now Princeton University, was the real pioneer of hymnody in the Presbyterian Church in America. He gave us the hymn "Lord, I am Thine, entirely Thine," one of the first of our truly evangelistic hymns, but, curiously, first finding favor in England before having any wide use in this country. This hymn (No. 224) is now to be found, among modern books, only in *The Methodist Hymnal*, although it was admitted to all Presbyterian hymnals prior to the last one, issued in 1933.

The controversy which began in various Presbyterian churches over the matter of strict adherence to Watts became a real issue in the question as to whether or not any hymns should be sanctioned. In time, as we know, the issue was decided in favor of the hymn.

The Baptists, at first little inclined toward any singing, used *The Bay Psalm Book* when they used anything at all. Their desire for sacramental hymns and their search for them led to their issuing *Hymns and Spiritual Songs* at Newport in 1766, the year Philip Embury and Robert Strawbridge began holding Methodist meetings. Opening with sixteen hymns on baptism, this book became the first truly denominational hymnal in America. Yet there was a decided preference among Baptists for a more popular type of church song. Their recruits came from uncultured groups gained through evangelistic methods; literary standards were not taken into account. Their preaching was highly emotional; and they wanted, and developed, a type of hymn in keeping with the character of the preaching—a fervid hymn which might be sung to a popular melody, preferably one with a refrain, or chorus. William Parkinson, who issued a *Selection* in 1809, remarked in the Preface to his book: "Songs have been circulated . . . which have been so barbarous in language, so unequal in numbers, so defective in rhyme, as to excite disgust in all persons even of tolerable understandings in these things; . . . so unsound in doctrine that no discerning Christian can sing or hear them without pain."

An example of the doggerel quite common to books of the period was the quaint "Christ the Appletree"—perhaps suggested by the allusion, "As the apple tree among the trees of the wood, so is my beloved among the sons," in the Song of Solomon (2:3). The first stanza ran:

> The tree of life, my soul hath seen,
> Laden with fruit, and always green;
> The trees of nature fruitless be,
> Compar'd with Christ the Appletree.

Following the general custom, many New England Baptist churches used Watts somewhat but insisted upon supplementing Watts with hymns of their own selection; it was in the South and the newly developing Middle West that Baptist hymnody ran riot.

Various groups holding Baptist views but not a part of the main body issued collections of hymns: the Freewill Baptists, the Universal Baptists, the Mennonites, The Church of God, the Disciples (the Campbellite Baptists), and other smaller groups all had their part in this activity, and the Presbyterians and Congregationalists were affected by it.

Whitefield's coming had stirred to its depths the religious groups in New England, and the resulting reaction was well-nigh universal in American churches. Booksellers and publishers were sensible to the demand for books and quickly responded to it; hymnbook making became an individual, frequently a commercial, enterprise. Nathan Strong, with assistants, brought out *The Hartford Selection*; Asahel Nettleton, who "never allayed the fears of enquirers," was responsible for *Village Hymns*; and Joshua Leavitt issued *The Christian Lyre*. Others, too numerous to mention, contributed offerings; but much of the material, sung to tunes which were mere repetitious jingles, had little or no literary merit. The Baptist groups were independent, individualistic, and submitted to no authority other than their own. They were hymnic anarchists.

But no more so than the Methodists. Sectarianism became rampant, and hymnody reflected denominational dogma. Methodists never reacted favorably to the hymns suggested by John Wesley; his "Sunday Service for America" never found a responsive echo in the heart of the American Methodist. While *The Pocket Hymn Book* and early editions of *The Methodist Hymnal* found places in the pews of the churches and in Methodist homes, their use was supplemented by other, semiofficial, books which were no improvement on those of other denominations—recall the hymn about the "O'Kellian minister recently turned Methodist" quoted earlier in this book. In fact, a Congregationalist minister confided to Joshua Leavitt while he was compiling his *Christian Lyre*: "We sacrifice too much to taste. The secret of the Methodists lies in the admirable adoption of their music to produce effect. . . . the moment we hear their ani-

mated, thrilling choruses we are electrified." In order to offset the inroads of the Unitarians, compilers of books which
had no official sanction "tinkered" with the older hymns in a
way which could not be sanctioned by any reasonable standard.

The camp meeting, from the year 1800, with its social
significance and its emphasis on singing, had a profound effect; only now are we becoming sincerely appreciative of
its real significance. Certain historians to the contrary notwithstanding, the history of this country cannot be properly or adequately presented without a great deal of attention's
being paid to the development of our frontiers as they opened
to the south and to the west. The camp meeting fostered
and further developed the type of folk hymn which had had
its beginnings earlier in New England. Death and destruction, hell-fire and damnation, were preached—"poured like
showers of rain," as the old Methodist hymn puts it. And the
texts of many other hymns reflect the same tendency as the
preaching; variants of the famous "Wicked Polly" hymn of
pre-Revolutionary days were common. As astonishing as it is
true, so late as 1883, in the *Western Record*, a hymnlike
poem, "An Awful Death," was printed. It begins,

> Come, sinner, hark! while I relate
> What happened in Kentucky state!
> A dear young woman lately died,
> And left behind her wealth and pride,

and goes on, ten stanzas in all, following closely the unfolding
of the "Wicked Polly" story hymn, which is worthy of being
quoted in full:

> O young people, hark! while I relate
> The story of poor Polly's fate!

She was a lady young and fair,
And died a-groaning in despair.

She would go to balls and dance and play,
In spite of all her friends could say;
"I'll turn," she said, "when I am old,
And God will then receive my soul":

One Sabbath morning she fell sick;
Her stubborn heart began to ache.
She cries, "Alas, my days are spent!
It is too late now to repent."

She called her mother to her bed,
Her eyes were rolling in her head;
A ghastly look she did assume;
She cried, "Alas! I am undone."

"My loving father, you I leave;
For wicked Polly do not grieve;
For I must burn for evermore.
When thousand thousand years are o'er.

"Your counsels I have slighted all,
My carnal appetite to fill.
When I am dead, remember well,
Your wicked Polly groans in hell."

She [w] rung her hands and groaned and cried
And gnawed her tongue before she died;
Her nails turned black, her voice did fail,
She died and left this lower vale.

May this a warning be to those
That love the ways that Polly chose,
Turn from your sins, lest you, like her,
Shall leave this world in black despair.

Charles Wesley's "Ah, lovely appearance of death," of finer literary texture yet a ghastly, lugubrious thing to us, maintained its place in all Methodist Episcopal hymnals until less than a century ago, and in the English *Wesleyan Hymn-Book* until its 1875 edition.

As is the case in folk verse generally, all sorts of homely subjects were dealt with. From early books—some of them from Boston!—were taken such things as "Miss Hathaway's Experience":

> That dareing sin I did commit,
> Was that, which some delight in yet,
> That heinous sin called civil mirth,
> God threatens with his dreadful curse.
> I often-times to church did go,
> My beauty and fine clothes to show.

Of course, she repented, was converted, and refused the appeal:

> My uncle said, don't be so dull,
> Come, go with me to yonder ball;
> I'll dress you up in silks so fine,
> I'll make you heir to all that's mine.

The foibles of women were a favorite subject, Mother Eve coming in for considerable attention, as this stanza will show:

> Can I forget the fatal deed,
> How Eve brought death to all her seed?
> She tasted the forbidden tree,
> Anger'd her God, and ruin'd me.

Denominationalism was stressed:

> Thus we have marched the ark around,
> And find no infants there;

If there are any to be found,
We wish to ask you where.

A good-sized book would be necessary were it to contain all of the "horrible examples" one might find. To be sure, the books of the type just mentioned contained better textual material than that quoted, much of it from Watts and Wesley; but when one searches for worth-while new contributions he has difficulty in finding any. He is reminded of another verse in the Song of Solomon: "I went down into the garden of nuts to see the fruits of the valley." The connotation is intriguing!

The Sunday- and day-school books of the period, used in the cities and towns, augmented the supply of religious singing books. One publisher, Horace Waters, issued hundreds of thousands of *The Sabbath School Bell*, typical of the small, end-fold books which came in a stream from all publishing houses which had facilities for printing music. One striking feature of these Sunday-school books is their cheerfulness, quite in contrast to the soberness and often lugubriousness of those for adults—"those of more mature minds," to use the language of good ritual. In them we find the joys of heaven anticipated, the satisfaction and even delight found in the Christian life. They were personal and subjective—"me" hymns which had in them little or nothing of the broader aspects of Christianity. There is little evidence of any social consciousness. Stephen Foster, of whom America is so proud, wrote hymns to be sung at the funeral services of children—one for little boys:

Little Willie's gone to heaven,
Praise the Lord!

> All his sins have been forgiven,
>   Praise the Lord!
>
> Joyful let your voices rise,
> Do not come with tearful eyes,
> Willie's dwelling in the skies;
>   Willie's gone to heaven;

and another for little girls:

> Little Ella's an angel in the skies,
>   Sing, merrily sing.
> Come brother and sister, cease your sighs,
>   Sing, merrily sing.
>
> Sing, merrily sing,
> Let the chorus joyfully ring!
> Ella's an angel in the skies,
>   Sing, merrily sing.

To children singing such verse, death couldn't be so terrible as it must have been to the children of earlier days who sang:

> Where shall a guilty child retire?
>   Forgotten and unknown?
> In hell I meet the dreadful fire;
>   In heaven the glorious throne.

Or this one among Charles Wesley's *Hymns for Children:*

> And am I only born to die?
> And must I suddenly comply
>   With nature's stern decree?
> What after death for me remains?
> Celestial joys, or hellish pains,
>   To all eternity!

167

The music of the little books was bright, catchy, and had an immediate appeal for children and adults alike.

From the more or less outlaw songs of the early days of our country—the songs from the singing schools, the folk hymns of the camp meeting (and earlier), and the Sunday-school songs just mentioned, especially the latter, came the much discussed and all-too-frequently cussed gospel song.

The reason for stressing the influence of the Sunday-school song on the gospel song should be obvious: songs learned in childhood carry over into adulthood. At a time when there were but one or two phases of religious thinking emphasized in our popular religious song, namely, the joys of heaven and the love of Christ for the person singing, this would prove particularly true. Then, too, there was little real difference in the texts and tunes of the Sunday-school books and the gospel songs. Each had a simple melody made easy to learn and recall by its equally simple harmonization; there were no rhythmic complications; and all were set to texts in common, everyday English familar to all. As the youngsters grew up and became the leaders in the churches, it was but natural they would favor the kind of song with which they had long been familiar, in many cases the only kind of song they knew. Many hardened sinners, too, joined lustily in singing such childish songs as

> Little drops of water,
> Little grains of sand,
> Make the mighty ocean
> And the pleasant land.

No honest, adequate history of the remarkable vogue of the gospel hymn has yet been written. It, perhaps, more than any other one thing, made America really music conscious. It constituted, as Waldo Selden Pratt has said, "a historic phenomenon." So far as its folklike characteristics were concerned, it was a welcome contrast to the old, solemn psalmody; and, as there was no other popular music worthy of mention to compete with it, it was sung by millions to whom more sophisticated music was a closed book. The number of gospel songbooks issued during the nineteenth century was about fifteen hundred, while the number of individual copies sold was enormous, those compiled by Ira D. Sankey alone reaching a sale of some fifty million. (In the ninety years between 1760 and 1850, some 275 tune books of the singing-school variety were issued; they came out at the rate of more than one each two weeks. This does not include word editions.) Such a sale constituted in itself a phenomenon, but more extraordinary was the effect upon the masses. There continues still a large use of gospel songbooks, but the number cannot be compared to that used by the members of the last two generations.

Many of the thousands of gospel songs published have been a distinct contribution to our hymnody because of their real worth; by no means should the whole movement be condemned. The type of song, however, that merely excites emotion, that has no point to it other than to give the singer a sense of physical well-being, that gets one all stirred up without impelling him to do anything about it, cannot be condemned too strongly. Yet let us not overlook the fact that our hymnals have been greatly strengthened, made more widely useful, by the inclusion of some of the best gospel songs, even though honest critics, on the basis of a superior taste in literature and music, will have none of them. Nevertheless, while they do not like them, they wisely do not ignore them.

True, during the whole period of the dominance of the gospel song, the various denominations continued issuing their several hymnals, while a number of commercial publishing houses issued collections of similar character. But they had no such widespread use as they have today; the gospel songbook was used in all of the services of the church except that of Sunday morning, while it almost wholly supplanted the use of the authorized hymnals in the homes. The denominational hymnals acted somewhat as a steadying influence; but, in large measure, they were looked upon as collections of sacred poetry rather than of verse to be sung.

The singing schools which used the books issued by Lowell Mason, Thomas Hastings, W. B. Bradbury, I. B. Woodbury, and a host of others during the nineteenth century played a large part in keeping before the people many of those hymns we like to call "standard." For they are a type quite apart from the gospel song, the texts being more restrained and the music more of the variety of the common hymn tune with which we have all become so familiar.

Another steadying influence was the hymn writing by those of Unitarian persuasion. We are sometimes surprised at the number of our best and most loved hymns which have been written by Unitarian poets. With them the literary motive was always strong, the humanitarian spirit in religion was emphasized, the relation of the worshiper to the indwelling Spirit was never lost sight of, and their main purpose seems always to have been the writing of hymns for congregational rather than liturgical use. American hymnody owes much to such Unitarian writers as Samuel Johnson,

Samuel Longfellow, Frederick Henry Hedge, Oliver Wendell Holmes, James Russell Lowell, and, among later writers, Frederick Lucian Hosmer and John Haynes Holmes. While anarchy reigned in the American hymnic world, it did not reign supreme.

With the coming of the twentieth century, men began to see more clearly; their religious thinking underwent a change; particularly was this true during and after the first World War. To be aware of the difference, one has but to consider the changed attitudes of the Christian world in the last twenty-five years and note the reflection of the changes in our latest hymnals: our present-day attitude toward missions; our greatly increased interest in the social gospel, in the brotherhood of men, in international affairs; and the waning of denominational emphasis. There is now evidence of an insight which, until this generation, had not been any too evident. We are told that today we have need of a "positive." May it not be found in our modern hymnals?

Men have recognized that people need spiritual reinforcement when passing through "fiery trials": may it not be found in the hymn "How firm a foundation" (No. 315)?

> "When through fiery trials thy pathway shall lie,
> My grace, all-sufficient, shall be thy supply,
> The flame shall not hurt thee; I only design
> Thy dross to consume, and thy gold to refine."

People need comforting in time of tribulation: "Lead, kindly Light" (No. 514).

> So long Thy power hath blest me, sure it still
> Will lead me on,
> O'er moor and fen, o'er crag and torrent, till
> The night is gone.

People need help in their daily lives: "Dear Master, in whose life I see" (No. 376).

> Though what I dream and what I do
> In my weak days are always two,
> Help me, oppressed by things undone,
> O Thou, whose deeds and dreams were one!

People need courage to keep up the battle for righteousness: "God of grace and God of glory" (No. 279).

> Grant us wisdom,
> Grant us courage,
> For the facing of this hour.[1]

People must have an outlet for their Christian energy: "Rise up, O men of God!" (No. 267).

> Rise up, O men of God!
> Have done with lesser things;
> Give heart and mind and soul and strength
> To serve the King of kings.[2]

People must have means of expressing thankfulness, and gratitude, and joy: "Angel voices, ever singing" (No. 15).

> Here, great God, today we offer
> Of Thine own to Thee;
> And for Thine acceptance proffer,
> All unworthily,
> Hearts and minds, and hands and voices
> In our choicest
> Melody.

Such needs cannot be met by mere doctrinal statements; by insisting on being only Methodists, or Presbyterians, or Baptists, or Congregationalists; by singing only of hell and damnation, or in contemplation of a home in heaven. If the Church is to satisfy those needs and to aid effectively in bringing in the Kingdom of God, it must have a deeper insight than that. Bishop Simpson, on an occasion, speaking of the task of the Church, said:

The Church must go into the field with the farmer, into the tent with the soldier, into the forecastle with the sailor, into the pit with the miner, into the counting room with the merchant; it must go into the alleys and purlieus of the city, and grope its way up the rickety stairs and kneel on the bare floor beside the loathsome sufferer. Like the atmosphere, it must press equally on all surfaces of society; like the sea, it must crowd into every nook of the shore line of humanity; like the sun, it must shine on things foul and low as well as things fair and high. For the Church was redeemed and organized and equipped and commissioned for the moral and spiritual renovation of the whole world.

That statement was in Calvin Weiss Laufer's thinking, so he told this writer, when he wrote his fine hymn beginning,

We thank Thee, Lord, Thy paths of service lead
To blazoned heights and down the slopes of need;
They reach Thy throne, encompass land and sea,
And he who journeys in them walks with Thee.[3] (No. 458.)

We have recognized the authority of established reputation and the force of opinion; we have suffered the confusion resulting from the assertion of individual liberty even to the point of license; we now seem to have developed the power of seeing into the situation as it is; we have gained intellectual discernment and penetration and understanding, have acquired a reflective knowing; we have come "from authority through anarchy to insight."

XI

THE ECUMENICAL TREND IN HYMNODY

A POSTSCRIPT TO A LETTER RECEIVED NOT LONG AGO SAID: "By the way, the word ecumenical is a good word and a new one to me." It may be new to many of us, but the word is really a very old one, coming from the Greek *oikoumenikos* —"the inhabited world"—which, in turn, came from *oikein* —"to inhabit"—and *oikos*—"house" or "dwelling." The latter and a derivative from *nemein* form the basis of our word "economy," originally meaning the management of domestic affairs. In its nonecclesiastical sense ecumenical means "general, world-wide in extent and influence," while in its strictly ecclesiastical sense it means "pertaining to, representing, or governing the whole Church." It is a good word, signifying, as it does, world-wide tolerance and liberality which is opposed to anything narrow or provincial. Inasmuch as the word connotes liberality, we are tending to accept "belonging to the whole Church" as its meaning.

The word was first applied in the ecclesiastical sense to the general councils of the early Church. In the Roman Church, the assembling of representatives from all parts of the world —those summoned from the whole Church—into a formal gathering which is presided over by the pope or by some accredited, properly delegated authority, is known as an ecumenical council.

While assemblies of churchmen called councils or synods

had been convened in the early centuries of the Church, it would appear that the Council of Nicaea was the first assembly of the Church Universal and so stands as the first ecumenical conference. The word until the present century has been used almost exclusively with reference to the affairs of the Roman Church, but it has now been taken over generally by other religious bodies—as, witness, the Ecumenical Methodist Conference, held for the first time in 1881. "The ecumenical movement, which is affecting the churches in matters concerning Faith and Order, Life and Work, and Missions, is having a comparable effect upon their worship," writes Dean Howard Chandler Robbins in the Preface to *Ecumenical Trends in Hymnody,* one of the "Pamphlet Library on Worship" issued by the Federal Council of Churches, an admirable little volume which he edited, and from which came the title of this chapter. Dean Robbins goes on to say:

If the Universal Church is regarded as a fellowship of those who worship God in Christ, then the increasing awareness of fellowship, the growing recognition of essential unity, is bound to find expression in prayer and praise.

. . . .

In the field of hymnody the most important effect of the growth in ecumenical consciousness is the enrichment which has already come through cross-fertilization.[1]

Following the illuminating Preface there are some sixty-odd pages of comments on the hymnody of the Methodists, the Lutherans, the Presbyterians, the Moravians, the Congregationalists, the Episcopalians, and—perhaps most interesting of all—the United Church of Canada. The last-named doubtless more nearly approaches the ecumenical ideal in hymnody than any of the others; for, while the Methodists have a book which was compiled by a Commission composed of representatives of its three largest groups, now united into one, while the Northern Baptist Convention and the Disciples of Christ have issued one jointly, that of the United Church of Canada is representative of a Church whose membership is made up of former members of several different denominations. In the case of the Methodists there were no doctrinal differences to overcome; such differences in the case of the others have apparently not stood as a barrier to their seeing eye to eye in their selection of common prayer and praise material for their hymnals.

An interesting side-light on how religious bodies are solving common problems, having nothing directly to do with the ecumenicity of hymnody, however, is the working arrangement which has recently been made between Chapman College, a Disciples' institution in California, and Whittier College, a Quaker one in the same state—the one definitely sacramentarian, the other as far from sacramentarianism as can be. In talking of this arrangement the new president of Chapman College stated that, while there would be a common chapel service for the students of both institutions, they would continue to worship on Sundays at their respective churches. When asked as to what hymnal they would use for their joint chapel services, President Reeves said that there should be no difficulty at all, that there were plenty of books from which they could sing together.

It is to be regretted that the Federal Council did not wait just a little longer before issuing this booklet in order that there might have been included comment on some excellent new hymnals which have been issued during the last few years. It is to be hoped there may be a second edition soon which may include essays on the new Lutheran book, for the Lutheran books discussed in the present edition are not the latest; that of the Evangelical and Reformed Church; the fine new *Mennonite Hymnary;* and that of the Baptists-Disciples, comparatively recently off the press.

While it was perhaps thought wise at the time the pamphlet was projected to include only denominational hymnals, a comparative study of the nondenominational books will, perhaps, show more definitely than any other study the real advance toward ecumenicity. Many are the churches which do not use their own denominational books; hundreds, probably thousands, of churches have supplemented their supply of denominational books with others for use in various departments of the churches. This is particularly true of the larger and stronger churches of most of our groups. However, because of this very thing we are talking about, the ecumenical trend, there is noticeably a tendency to use the denominational book more and more in such situations. It is being discovered that, very generally speaking, the denominational books have as wide a selection of material as the others. The various books even look so much alike that after one is once opened the worshiper feels quite at home in using it, forgetting whether it is bound in red or blue cloth!

After all, hymns have always been ecumenical in character. This is said advisedly, for the rhymed lines showing denominational bias which appeared in most of our denominational hymnals a few generations ago were not hymns at all. They were not songs "with praise of God," to quote St. Augustine, or sacred verse which might fall within the wider definition of a hymn as set forth in one of the recent Hymn

Society papers prepared by Carl Price. They were rhymed praise of the particular sect to which the author belonged. Dean Robbins states it quietly, soberly, and adequately: "Hymns which are exaggerated or one-sided in their doctrinal emphasis do not come into general use, and sooner or later are discarded."

Gregory the Great, after the organization of the early Church hymnody, was firmly of the conviction that all that was needed to make the whole world Christian was to have it sing the same songs in the same way. While he and his immediate successors were unable to carry out the plan because of differences in the Church, especially the controversy with the Lombards, when Charlemagne was called by Pope Adrian to straighten out political and ecclesiastical difficulties, the new emperor went at the business of establishing an ecumenical hymnody with a vengeance. Not all of his tactics were as ethical as might have been desired; yet he was active, aggressive, and in considerable measure successful.

The Lutheran hymnody, which has always had such high regard for God's Word, may be thought of as being ecumenical in character if we recognize that it has never been narrow in the strictly denominational sense—that is, in the sense in which much of it could not be used by any sect other than the Roman Catholic. Such is also true of the emphasis of the Calvinists on the singing of psalms, and of a very great deal which came from the brain and hand of Isaac Watts, Charles Wesley, and the host of their imitators and followers. And in the case of the transition from psalmody to hymnody in the "free" churches it is especially noticeable. Most, if not all, of the forward movements in the evolution of our hymnody have been ecumenical in character. There has never been anything denominational in the character of the music to which the hymns have been sung, even though the popular, then new, tunes which were sung with such gusto during the Wesleyan Revival in England were referred to derisively as "old Methodist tunes."

James T. Lightwood, English authority on hymn tunes, in one of his books, *Hymn Tunes and Their Story*, has a chapter headed "A Chat About 'Old Methodist Tunes,'" which he opens with this statement:

Old prejudices die hard, and in psalmody no illusion is harder to dispel than the mistaken idea that the tunes which are understood by the above title in any way represent the hymn-tunes of the early Methodists. . . . the tunes under notice here belong to no particular section of the church, but are to be found in the tune-books of the Church of England, Baptists, Methodists, Independents, and even Roman Catholics during a period of some seventy years from about 1780, while the period of production may be reckoned from 1780 to 1830.

So, even in that period of controversy, there is no doubt that the tunes which were sung in divine worship were common property.

In his admirable collection, *Christ in Song*, Philip Schaff says:

It is remarkable how Christians occupying different sections in the great family unite in choosing the same words in which to utter His praise;

and he might well have added, "the same music." He continues:

The hymns of Jesus are the Holy of holies in the temple of sacred poetry. From this sanctuary every doubt is banished; here the passions of sense, pride, and unholy ambition give way to the tears of penitence, the joys of faith, the emotions of love, the aspirations of hope, the anticipations of heaven; here the dissentions of rival churches and theological schools are hushed into silence; here the hymnists of ancient, mediaeval and modern times, from every section of Christendom—profound divines, stately bishops, humble monks, faithful pastors, devout laymen, holy women—all unite with one voice in the common adoration of a common Saviour. He is the theme of all ages, tongues, and creeds, the divine harmony of all human discords, the solution of all the dark problems of life.

As Louis F. Benson has said,

It is . . . important to remember that in the mind of the plain, everyday Christian, where feeling conditions reflection so strongly, the hymns he uses devotionally, and especially those he loves, do more to form his religious thinking than anything else except the Bible.[2]

And C. J. Abbey, in an essay on English sacred poetry of the eighteenth century, wrote:

It may be said to be the peculiar privilege of hymn-writers that to a great extent they write, not for any society of Christians, but for the Church at large. Men whose theological views contrast most strongly meet on common ground when they express in verse the deeper aspirations of the heart, and the choice of Christian praise.[3]

Christians of all denominations have been meeting in our hymnals for hundreds of years.

As the ecumenical movement has enriched modern hymnody, so too, modern hymnody has its contribution to make and that a very important one, to the ecumenical movement, says Dean Robbins. An actual occurrence which will bear out this statement may be of interest. Undoubtedly the Methodist common interest in a common book did much to bring about the union of the three largest bodies of that denomination in 1939. Only four years after the first aggressive attempt to bring the matter of unification to a vote of the various conferences of the Methodist Episcopal Church and the Methodist Episcopal Church, South—at which time the movement was decisively defeated, largely because of the influence of two strong men—the first of three commissions to revise *The Methodist Hymnal* was appointed by one of the groups. Two others joined the movement by appointing their respective commissions, and the three worked together for five years in perfect concord to bring forth the latest offering of the Methodists. In that joint group, comprised of many of the leading representatives of the three Churches, the men got to know each other personally; some of them had been diametrically opposed to each other in the attempt to bring about union. They discovered, through studying and singing hymns together that, as one good man of one of the groups stated it, "we are all Methodists; we are all Christians; we are all gentlemen, I hope; is there any reason why we should not see eye to eye?" One of the two men who were probably most influential in bringing about the defeat of the union of the Methodist bodies in 1924 stated privately to this writer that, although he could not bring himself, personally, to favor union, for reasons which he felt to be good and sufficient so far as he was concerned (and they were!), he would not aggressively oppose it longer; his experience with others in this commission work had shown him, as nothing else had been able to make him see, that when people sing together the great hymns of their faith in the spirit of those great hymns, they cannot be far apart so far as their Christian living and their desire to bring in the Kingdom is concerned.

In 1930 Frank A. Morgan compiled a book called the *Inter-Church Hymnal,* using unusual methods in gathering his materials, both hymns and tunes. He sought the verdict of hymn users before, instead of after, publication through contacts he made with more than ten thousand ministers located in the various states of the Union. From church bulletins submitted by these ministers 325 hymns were selected as representative of the national taste in hymns, for each one of the 325 had been "sung and repeated by from ten per cent to ninety-five per cent of the churches reporting."

The tunes used were passed upon favorably by 650 Fellows or Associate Fellows of the American Guild of Organists.

The hymns appear in the order sung by the greatest number of churches. This, of course, admitted of no system of classification, and is a weakness of the book. Another weakness is that of having had the tunes approved only by the more musically learned members of the A.G.O.—it gives only the viewpoint of the organist, not always a singer or the best judge of what constitutes good singing material. However, it was an interesting experiment and some valuable data were gathered. Could there be such a thing as an ecumenical survey, this was one.

Statistics are not always impressive; one may prove too many things by the same figures. But some results of a limited survey of nine late hymnals—seven of them denominational ones—should be interesting if not profitable. Comparison, hymn by hymn and tune by tune, was made of the first thirty of those given in the *Inter-Church Hymnal* in order that it might be discovered how nearly the churches were together in the matter of association of hymn and tune. The study might have gone further, perhaps with profit; but the work became too monotonous—there was too much sameness to make it interesting.

The books selected were the new hymnals of the Baptists and Disciples, Congregationalists, Methodists, Mennonites, Presbyterians, Lutherans (Missouri Synod), and that of the Evangelical and Reformed Church as well as the nondenominational *New Hymnal of Praise*, edited by Edward Dwight Eaton, 1941, and *Worship in Song*, edited by Caroline B. Parker, 1942.

It was not to be expected that all of the hymns in the list would be found in the Lutheran *Hymnal*—not if one had read Dr. Reed's statement in the booklet *Ecumenical Trends in Hymnody* (p. 34) that,

> gospel hymns and other light or sentimental hymns and tunes are not included. We also look in vain for hymns of the vague and nonchurchly type represented by the New England poets of Quaker of Unitarian connection. . . . By the same token no welcome has been extended to the large and attractive body of national folk songs. Ar Hyd y Nos, Ton-y-Botel, Finlandia and many such, will be sought in vain.

But of the more than twenty which are common to all of the books considered, we find our Lutheran brethren sing the same tunes to the hymns the other denominations use except in three cases, these being different tunes to "How firm a foundation," "Love divine, all loves excelling," and "Jesus calls us, o'er the tumult." Following the Harvard departure of using only the old camp-meeting tune, "Foundation" (it is *not* by Anne Steele), to "How firm a foundation," the Baptists and Disciples use it alone while all others use *"Adeste Fidelis"* (Portuguese Hymn). The Methodists and Congregationalists use "Geibel" to "Stand up, stand up for Jesus"; all others "Webb" (as is proper). The Evangelical and Reformed, Lutheran, and Presbyterian books, as well as that of Miss Parker, chose "Hanover" for "O worship the King," the others using "Lyons." The Methodists are the only ones who sing anything other than "Hamburg" to "When I survey the wondrous cross"; they use "Eucharist." They should use "Hamburg." We stand on even ground in the use of "Dennis" or "Boylston" to "Blest be the tie that binds," but each is so very familiar that it doesn't make much difference which one is used.

And one is impressed by the hymnic ecumenicity when he discovers the Congregationalists were willing to desert Watts to follow John Wesley! They sing "O God, our help in ages past"; but the Presbyterians, Lutherans, and Evangelical and Reformed brethren cling to the original, "Our God, our help," and so forth.

One thing is difficult to understand: why does our ecumenicity not extend to the naming of our hymn tunes? We are all offenders in that respect, although some editors seem to go out of their way to be different. One wonders, for instance, why the well-known tune "He leadeth Me" should ever be called "Aughton," as is the case in some instances. But like the ways of a maid with a man, the ways of hymnbook editors in respect to the naming of tunes are unfathomable. The editor of one book, *Sursum Corda,* some years ago changed most of the names of the tunes he used—so many, in fact, that he found it necessary to include an extra index to note the changes he had made. Referring to the annoyance caused by duplication of names for tunes, Dean Lutkin once said: "This duplication of names makes much trouble for the hymn-tune researcher. If the authentic name of a tune is not at hand, the average hymn-book compiler will invent a name of his own rather than go to any trouble in the matter." [4] Dean Lutkin was far from an "average" compiler; yet he and Karl Harrington did some strange things by way of naming tunes in the 1905 *Methodist Hymnal*, of which they were the musical editors. Here is one place, at least, where we should really get together, and at once.

The little excursion into the statistical field also showed some further ecumenical tendencies in our changing tune preferences. Where in the 1905 edition of *The Methodist Hymnal* and the 1911 Presbyterian *Hymnal* there were, respectively, 49 and 60 tunes by J. B. Dykes, 51 and 35 by Joseph Barnby, and 17 and 22 by Arthur Sullivan, the recent editions of the same books show, again respectively, 28 and 25 by Dykes, 13 and 11 by Barnby, and 11 and 6 by Sullivan. The tendency toward getting away from the tunes of the late-nineteenth-century English organists is found also in the other newer books with the exception of that edited by Dr. Henry Hallam Tweedy, *Christian Worship and Praise*. He has used 42 tunes by Dykes, 26 by Barnby, and 16 by Sullivan. Allowance has not been made for duplications in any of the cases cited. The general trend is toward the use of more chorale-type tunes; those from the older psalters; folklike tunes; and some plain song, more often than not in modified form. It is peculiarly gratifying to realize that we are thinking alike musically in our hymn singing.

Noticeable is the fact that the whole movement in hymn

writing in America has been even more ecumenical in character than has been the case in other countries. France is definitely Catholic; Germany *was* either strongly Protestant or Catholic; England, even though the home of the "free" sects, has never been able to get out from under the great influence of the Anglican Church. But in this country there has been no greatly predominating denomination. This, perhaps, has had much to do with the development of hymn writing happily free from traditional influences and barriers. George T. Rider had this interesting thing to say in the Preface to his *Lyra Americana:*

Our religious poetry lacks that deep historical back-ground of ecclesiastical architecture and tradition—that rich liturgical usage and feeling which lend so many grave and varied splendors of ripeness, mystery, color, and tone to the English school. It is wanting, too, in the congruity and unity that in a large degree flow from these broad influences. Neither do we behold that steady flow of style, born of high polish and consummate discipline, cherished in the University life.

It should be said that Rider was writing at a time when the hymnbooks used in this country were quite denominationally inclined; that is, there were easily noticed, frequently quite evident, denominational distinctions such as have been referred to as "rhymed lines." However, soon after the Civil War such distinctions began rapidly to disappear and by the opening of this century had all but disappeared so far as they had any effect at all on the writing of hymns.

Say what we will of the gospel song, it had a tremendous influence in bending, if not breaking through, denominational lines. All members of different denominations sang the same songs, and people began to feel somewhat at home in churches other than their own when they visited them.

The carols which now grace all of our hymnals have never been anything but ecumenical in character.

Henry Wilder Foote in his excellent book *Three Centuries of American Hymnody,* while in no way referring to what Rider had to say about the "high polish and consummate discipline, cherished in the University life," does call attention to the leadership in hymn writing in our country of men from Harvard, Yale, and Andover. He speaks particularly of the excellent hymnbooks compiled by Harvard men over the last century and a half, of the quality of the hymns they have written, and of the number who have made contributions of hymns. He says:

> In this respect no other institution in the English-speaking world can compare with Harvard, save Trinity College, Cambridge, England. . . . The writers belonged by blood, by education, and by social ties to the New England literary group. They were set down in Harvard as impressionable young men at a period when the spirit of the time was most favorable to the stimulation of poetic gifts. They had the culture, the familiarity with literary methods, and the warmth of atmosphere needed. And, happily, the greatest writers did not come first, to overshadow and check men with lesser gifts, as Watts overshadowed the Independents in England, and Charles Wesley the Methodists; nor were they dominated by the greater tradition of the Church of England, as were the American Episcopalians whose needs were satisfied by the Anglican hymn writers.[5]

We may pardon the bouquets thrown to Harvard men, for the lectures which comprise this book were given at the time Harvard was celebrating her tercentennial anniversary; but what he says is true and of significance. Especially is it significant that the earlier hymn writers in this country were not among the greatest—they were not overshadowed by men of greater gifts. Then, too, Harvard has ever been a liberal institution, "under no bonds to keep within the limits of an established creed or ritual." She was able to provide leadership which gave us a hymnic product with no denominational leaning.

In the compilation of his book Rider says he undertook

to gather in the best sacred verses from all available sources, entirely irrespective of Doctrinal or Ecclesiastical affinities, or individual preferences;—verses breathing something of a common Catholicity, while representing the Lyric spirit of our different communions.

While *Lyra Americana* is a book of religious poetry, it is not a book of hymns, as such. There is, of course, much religious poetry that is not suitable for use as hymns, as we all know. However, this book has had quite a little influence on the thinking of hymnbook compilers.

Stanley A. Hunter has said:

No denominational lines are drawn in our hymnals, and in the praise of the sanctuary we have already an expression of real unity.[6]

As to the music element in hymnody, F. J. Gillman has this to say:

And there is yet another debt which religion owes to music. It is independent of sects and creeds and tongues. The historic creeds, intended in their inception "to remove all grounds of difference and to wind up by laws of peace every link of controversy," (Emperor Constantine's speech at the opening of the Council of Nicaea) have, as a matter of history, placed stumbling blocks in the way of the very cause they were meant to serve. They are divisive, but music is unifying.[7]

188

Referring to the contribution which the hymn has made to the cause of Christian reunion, Gillman continues:

In its poetry the Church discovers a unity which reaches down below creedal differences. The creeds are like the troubled waves on the surface of the waters; the love of which the poets sing is like the undivided ocean below. It is indeed refreshing, as we study our hymnals, to realize that here we can turn aside from controversy, and, forgetting our differences, can attain a true unity of the spirit in a glad fraternity of praise. And this unity overlaps national as well as ecclesiastical barriers. Through the medium of the music and the translations which skilled hands and loving hearts have made we can commune with our fellow-Christians of many lands, even though we cannot speak their tongue. Above the tumult of hatreds and wars, these songs rise from many lips to Him who is the Father of us all.[8]

Edward Caldwell Jones said:

A hymn . . . implies a body of worshippers. It expresses a common feeling which seeks and finds fulfillment in the joy or pain, the love and hope, of others.[9]

Encouraging is the fact that the newer compilations of hymns for young people know nothing of denominational lines—they are ecumenical in fact. Only recently have we had such books. Most of our early American books either had no hymns at all for young people or offered them hymns of such doleful character that one wonders how they ever had the slightest attraction for anyone, especially young folks.

The union of the churches in Canada, that of the Methodists in this country and in England as well, that of the Evangelical and Reformed churches, the spirit of unity shown by the Baptists and Disciples in their joining in issuing a hymnal, the very definite trend toward union in the denominations in our country, and the amazing change of front which is noted among certain leaders of the Anglican Church are all indications that the Christian world is thinking ecumenically.

In our hymnals there will always be, of course, certain preferences. One would not expect, or want, the Methodists to omit "And are we yet alive?" or "And let our bodies part"; nor would we expect any other denomination than the Congregationalists to include

> The breaking waves dashed high
> On a stern and rock-bound coast.

There is a feeling that if the Christian people of America were able to speak with one voice, through one religious organization, what they might have to say would receive much more respect in high secular places than does their present divided speech; for one strong voice backed by sixty million people would be much more effective than a number of voices —lesser voices. The old fable of the fagots applies here.

But our hymnody may be a leaven which is working quietly, unceasingly, toward the bringing about of an organic union among our churches which may be a greater factor in determining the future course of events in this world than we now dream.

REFERENCES

I. WHAT IS WORSHIP?

1. Harry Webb Farrington. Copyright 1921. Used by permission of Mrs. Harry Webb Farrington.

II. WHAT IS A HYMN?

1. The Abingdon Press, 1932, p. 15.
2. *Ibid.*, p. 9.
3. Arthur E. Gregory, *The Hymn-Book of the Modern Church*, London, Charles H. Kelly, 1904, p. 8.
4. *Ibid.*, p. 10.
5. John Ellerton, *Principles of Hymn-Book Construction.*
6. Gregory, *op. cit.*, p. 17.
7. Used by permission of Dean Earl Marlatt.
8. I Esdras 4:41.

III. PAGAN SOURCES?

1. John F. Rowbotham, *History of Music*, Charles Scribner's Sons, 1899.
2. James Baikie, "Hymns (Egyptian)," *Encyclopaedia of Religion and Ethics*, ed. James Hastings, Charles Scribner's Sons, 1928, VII, 38.
3. Adolf Erman, *Life in Ancient Egypt*, London, Macmillan & Co., 1894, p. 391.
4. Adolf Erman, *A Handbook of Egyptian Religion*, New York, E. P. Dutton & Co., Inc., 1907, p. 48.
5. James Henry Breasted, *The Dawn of Conscience*, Charles Scribner's Sons, 1933, p. 282.
6. Ralph T. H. Griffith, *Hymns of the Rig-Veda.*

7. William Dwight Whitney, *Oriental and Linguistic Studies,* Charles Scribner's Sons.
8. J. Murdoch, *An Account of the Vedas.*
9. Max Müller, *India, What Can It Teach Us?* Longmans, Green & Co.
10. Arthur Anthony Macdonell, *History of Sanskrit Literature,* D. Appleton & Co.
11. *The Wisdom of the Hindus,* ed. Brian Brown, Brentano's, 1921. Garden City Publishing Co.
12. See H. Julius Eggeling, *Sacred Books of the East.*
13. See E. Vernon Arnold, *The Rig-Veda.*
14. Horace Hayman Wilson, *Translation of the Rig-Veda Sanhitâ.*
15. Murdoch, *op. cit.*
16. *Ibid.*
17. E. D. Soper, *The Religions of Mankind,* Abingdon-Cokesbury Press, 1940, p. 108.
18. Reprinted from Cumming, *The Assyrian and Hebrew Hymns of Praise,* by permission of Columbia University Press.
19. Hugo Radau, *Sumerian Hymns and Prayers,* Department of Archaeology, University of Pennsylvania, 1911.
20. Cumming, *op. cit.*

IV. THE PSALMS

1. *The Hymnal,* Presbyterian Board of Christian Education, 1936.

V. CHANTS AND CANTICLES

1. John Telford, *New Methodist Hymn-Book Illustrated,* London, Epworth Press, 1934.
2. Nolan B. Harmon, Jr., *The Rites and Ritual of Episcopal Methodism,* Abingdon-Cokesbury Press, 1926, p. 150.
3. Gregory, *op. cit.*
4. *Church Club Lectures,* 1862.

VI. EARLY GREEK AND LATIN HYMNS

1. *Hymns of the Eastern Church,* London, J. T. Hayes, 1876.
2. Richard Chevenix Trench, *Sacred Latin Poetry,* London, Macmillan & Co., 1873.

VII. LATER LATIN HYMNS AND SEQUENCES

1. Used by permission of James B. Naylor.
2. Trench, *op. cit.*
3. Samuel W. Duffield, *Latin Hymns,* Funk & Wagnalls, 1899.
4. *Life of Notker.*

VIII. CHORALES AND METRICAL PSALMS

1. Miles Coverdale, *Goostly Psalms and Spir40*e Songes,* 1539
   (?).
2. Charles Stanley Phillips, *Hymnody, Past and Present,* The Macmillan Co., 1937.

X. OUR AMERICAN HERITAGE AND CONTRIBUTION

1. Used by permission of Harry Emerson Fosdick.
2. Used by permission of *The Presbyterian Tribune,* formerly *The Presbyterian Advance.*
3. Used by permission of the author and the Presbyterian Board of Christian Education.

XI. THE ECUMENICAL TREND IN HYMNODY

1. This and other quotations from *Ecumenical Trends in Hymnody,* edited by Dean Howard Chandler Robbins, are used by permission of the Federal Council of the Churches of Christ in America.
2. L. F. Benson, *The Hymnody of the Christian Church,* Harper & Bros., 1927. Dr. Benson's monumental *The English Hymn* should be in the libraries of all who are interested in the serious study of hymns.
3. Quoted by Francis T. Palgrave, *The Treasury of Sacred Song,* Oxford, The Clarendon Press, 1892.
4. Peter C. Lutkin, *Music in the Church,* Morehouse-Gorham Co., 1910.
5. Harvard University Press, 1940. Reprinted by permission of the President and Fellows of Harvard College.

6. *Music and Religion*, ed. Stanley A. Hunter, The Abingdon Press, 1930.
7. *The Evolution of the English Hymn*, The Macmillan Co., 1927.
8. *Ibid.*
9. *Harvard University Hymn Book.* Reprinted by permission of the President and Fellows of Harvard College.

INDEX OF HYMNS, STANZAS, SONGS

First Lines or Titles

A charge to keep I have, 22
A mighty fortress is our God, 125
Abide with me, 71
Ah, lovely appearance of death, 165
Alleluia, for the Lord God omnipotent reigneth, 89
All glory, laud, and honor, 107
All hail the power of Jesus' name, 16
All my heart this night rejoices, 127, 150
All people that on earth do dwell, 70, 137
All praise to Thee, my God, this night, 142
All things come of Thee, 66
Amen, that is, so let it be, 80
Among the smooth Moravians, 30
Angel voices, ever singing, 151, 172
And am I only born to die? 167
And are we yet alive? 190
And let our bodies part, 190
"Are ye able?" said the Master, 29
Art thou weary, art thou languid, 98
As with gladness men of old, 151
Awake, my soul, and with the sun, 142
Awake, thou that sleepest, 89

Before Thy throne, O Lord of Heaven, 32
Be not ashamed, I warrande thee, 136
Be still, my soul: the Lord is on thy side, 150
Blessed Jesus, at Thy word, 129
Blessing, and glory, and wisdom, 89
Blest be the tie that binds, 184
Brief life is here our portion, 109

Can I forget the fatal deed? 165
Christian! dost thou see them? 98
Christ is now risen agayne, 121
Christ ist erstanden, 120
Christ the Lord is risen today, 116
Come, Holy Ghost, our hearts inspire, 110
Come, Holy Spirit, heavenly Dove, 115
Come, sinner, hark! while I relate, 163
Come, ye faithful, raise the strain, 98

Dear Lord and Father of mankind, 49
Dear Master, in whose life I see, 172
Dies Irae, 116-17

Ein' feste Burg, 124-25, 136

Father of Jesus Christ, my Lord, 35
Fierce was the wild billow, 96
Fight the good fight, 151
For thee, O dear, dear country, 109-10
Fröhlich soll mein Herze springen, 127
From all that dwell below the skies, 143

Gloria in excelsis Deo, 76
Gloria, laus et honor, 107
Glory be to the Father, 78
Glory to God in the highest, 75-76
God of grace and God of glory, 172
Grant us wisdom, 172
Guilt no longer can distress me, 128

Hail, gladdening Light, 85
Hail thee, Festival Day! 106

Hark! the herald angels sing, 147-48

Here, great God, today we offer, 172

Holy, holy, holy Lord God of Hosts, 32

Holy Spirit, Truth divine, 115

Honor and glory, power and salvation, 89

Hora novissima, 109

How firm a foundation, 171, 183-84

I know not how that Bethlehem's Babe, 16

I love to steal awhile away, 71

I'll praise my Maker while I've breath, 140

I'm gonna ride upon a cloud, 32

In the cross of Christ I glory, 25

In the Garden, 32

In the midst of life we are in death, 114

In the resorts of Bardesanes, 91

Jerusalem the golden, 109-10

Jesu dulcis memoria, 107

Jesus calls us, o'er the tumult, 183

Jesus Christ is risen today, 116

Jesus, Lover of my soul, 35, 131

Jesus shall reign where'er the sun, 144

Jesus, still lead on, 131, 150

Jesus, Thou joy of loving hearts, 108

Jesus, Thy blood and righteousness, 131

Jesus, Thy boundless love to me, 128

Joy to the world, 144

King David and King Solomon, 105

Lauda Sion, 116

Lead, kindly Light, 71, 151, 171

Let all mortal flesh keep silence, 99

Let all the world in every corner sing, 143, 154

Life of ages, richly poured, 37

Lift up your heads, ye mighty gates, 127

Little drops of water, 168

Little Ella's an angel in the skies, 167

Little Willie's gone to heaven, 166

Lord, have mercy upon us, 118

Lord, I am Thine, entirely Thine, 160

Lord, now lettest Thy servant depart in peace, 77

Love divine, all loves excelling, 183

May the grace of Christ our Saviour, 115

Media vita in morte sumus, 114

My God, I love Thee, 111

My Jesus, as Thou wilt, 130

Never further than Thy cross, 84

Now thank we all our God, 126, 150

Now unto the King eternal, 89

Nun danket alle Gott, 126

O all ye works of the Lord, 79

O be joyful in the Lord, 69

O come, let us sing unto the Lord, 67

O come, O come, Immanuel, 111

O day of rest and gladness, 151

O filii et filiae, 118

O gladsome Light, 86

O God, our help in ages past, 36, 144, 184

O God, our Light! to Thee we bow, 32

O go your way into His gates, 70

O grant that nothing in my soul, 128

O happy home, where Thou art loved the dearest, 132, 150

O Jesu Christ, mein schönstes Licht, 128

O Jesus, I have promised, 151

O sacred Head now wounded, 108

O Son of God incarnate, 35

O Spirit of the Living God, 115

O splendor of God's glory bright, 103

O Thou, to whose all-searching sight, 131

O Thou who camest from above, 35

O Will of God beneath our life, 35

O worship the King, 184

INDEX OF HYMNS, STANZAS, SONGS

O young people, hark! while I relate, 163

Of Him who did salvation bring, 108

Onward, Christian soldiers, 151

Open wide upon her lap . . . , 156

Our God, our help in ages past, 184

Praise God, from whom all blessings flow, 142

Praise to the Lord, the Almighty, the King of Creation, 129, 150

Present with us ever be the Holy Spirit's grace, 114

Ride on! ride on in majesty!, 148

Rise up, O men of God, 172

Salve, festa dies, 106

Sancti Spiritus adsit nobis gratia, 114

Saviour, again to Thy dear name we raise, 18, 151

Shepherd of tender youth, 92

Sing praise to God who reigns above, 150

So long Thy power hast blest me, sure it still, 171

Spirit of faith, come down, 115

Spirit of Life, in this new dawn, 115

Splendor paternae gloriae, 103

Stabat mater dolorosa, 116-17

Stand up, stand up for Jesus, 184

Teach me, my God and King, 142

That dareing sin I did commit, 165

The breaking waves dashed high, 190

The day is past and over, 96

The day of resurrection, 98

The Church with psalms must shout, 101

The Church's one foundation, 151

The King of love my Shepherd is, 141, 151

The royal banners forward go, 106

The spacious firmament on high, 144

The strife is o'er, 118

The tree of life, my soul hath seen, 161

The world is very evil, 109-10

There is a land of pure delight, 24

There's not a bonnie flower that springs, 34

There's not a strain to memory dear, 34

Thou hidden love of God, 131

Though what I dream and what I do, 172

Thus we have marched the ark around, 165

To the Name that is salvation, 111

Veni, Creator Spiritus, 110, 114-15

Veni, Sancte Spiritus, 116

Vexilla Regis prodeunt, 106

Victimae paschali, 116

Wake Israel from his sleep, O Lord, 128

We plow the fields and scatter, 132

We praise Thee, O God, 84

We thank Thee, Lord, Thy paths of service lead, 173

Welcome, day of the Lord, 106, 111

Welcome, happy morning, 106

When all Thy mercies, O my God, 144

When I survey the wondrous cross, 184

When through fiery trials thy pathway shall lie, 171

Where shall a guilty child retire? 167

Worthy is the Lamb, 89

Yet has Christ a need of me, 103

GENERAL INDEX

Abbey, C. J., 180
Addison, Joseph, 144
Adonis, 45
Adrian, Pope, 178
Advent, 111, 116, 127
Agni, Hymn to, 53
Ainsworth, Henry, 156-57
Akkadian (-s), 55
Alden, John, 156
Alexander, James W., 108
Alexandria, 73, 91
Alleluia, 79, 112-13
Ambo, 112
Ambrose, 62, 82, 92, 100-3, 115, 120
Amen, 79-81
America, 62
American Guild of Organists, 182
"An Awful Death," 163
Ancient Art of Poetic Improvisation, The, 89
Andover, 187
"Angelic Song," 76, 78
Anglican Church, 68, 111, 186
Antioch, 62, 89
"Antiphon," 143
Apocalypse, 72
Apocrypha, 79
Arianism, 78, 91-92, 99-100
Arion, 73
Arius, 90-91
Arrian, 11
Aryan man, 48
Aryans, 39, 51-52
Asbury, Bishop, 108
Asiatic religions, old, 57
Assyria, 55
Assyrian hymns and poetry, 58
Athanasius, 69, 91

Atharva-Veda, 49, 51
Augustine, 22-23, 27, 36, 82, 92, 108, 122, 131, 177
Authorized Version, 63
Auxentius, 100

Babylonia, 55
Bach, Johann Sebastian, 125
Baker, Sir Henry William, 141, 151
Baptists (Northern Convention), 65
Bardesanes, 91
Baring-Gould, Sabine, 151
Barnby, Sir Joseph, 152, 185
Barton, William, 139
Bay Psalm Book, 157-58, 160
Benedicamus Domino, 118
Benedictine editors, 103
Benedicite, 79, 81
Benedictus, 69, 72, 75
Benson, Hugh, 12
Benson, Louis F., 71, 103, 117, 180
Bernard of Clairvaux, 107-9
Bernard of Cluny, 109-10
Bible
  Acts 4, 78
  Colossians 3:16, 36
  Corinthians, I
    13, 78
    14:26, 88
  Deuteronomy 32:7, 93
  Ephesians 5:14, 89
  Luke
    1:46-55, 74
    1:68-79, 69, 75
    2:14, 75
    2:29-32, 77
    15:5, 141
  Psalms
    2, 78

199

Psalms—*Continued*
  19, 144
  23, 140, 141
  36, 144
  46, 136
  48, 79
  72, 144
  84, 140
  92, 68, **70**
  95, 68
  98, 144
  100, 68-69, **71, 137**
  104, 46, 47
  117, 144
  130, 68
  148, 23
Song of Solomon
  2:3, 161
  6:11, 166
Timothy, I, **1:17, 89**
Revelation
  5:12, 89
  7:12, 89
  19:6, 89
Blue Laws, 145
Bode, J. E., 151
Bohemian Brethren, 121
Böhler, Peter, 130
Bonar, Horatius, 92, 148
Bonum est, 68, 70
Book of Common Prayer, 63, 69-70,
  75, 77, 79, 138, 152
Book of the Dead, 48
Borthwick, Jane L., 150
Bourgeois, Louis, 137
Bowring, John, 25
Boyce in D, 68
Boyce, William, 68
Bradburn, Samuel, 35
Bradbury, W. B., 170
Brahmanas, 51
Brahmans, 48, 50-51
Brattle Street Church, 158-59
Brewer, Bishop Leigh H., 76
"Brewing of Soma, The," 49
Bridges, Robert, 103

Brown, Brian, 50
Browne, Simon, 139
Brownlie, John, 110
Browning, Elizabeth Barrett, 94
Burns, Robert, 34

Calendar, Church, 149
Call to Worship, 69
Calvinism (-ists), 132, 134, 136-37,
  178
Calvin, John, 62, 132-38
Camp meeting, The, 163
"Candlelight Hymn," 86
Canonical hours, 94
Canons at Lauds, 94
Carol, old French, 76
Carol (-s), 118, 187
Caswall, Edward, 108, 150
Chaldea, 56
Chaldeans, 55
Chandler, John, 103
Chandragupta, 50
Chanting, 64 ff.
  antiphonal, 101
Chapman College, 176
Charlemagne, 114, 178
Charles, Elizabeth R., 84, 92
Charles II, 142
Charles the Bald, 114
Charles Wesley, Evangelist and Poet, 21
Chaucer, Geoffrey, 138
Cherubic Hymn, 99
Chorale, 122-25
Christian Century, The, 34
*Christian Hymns of the First Three
  Centuries,* 90
Christian Lyre, The, 162
Christian Year, 148
Christian   Worship   and   Praise
  (Tweedy), 185
Christ in Song, 179
Christmas, 118, 121
"Christ the Appletree," 161
Chrysostom, 92
Church Club, New York, 81
Festal (chanting), **66**

Church fathers, 62, 90, 99
Church of England (*see also* English Church), 63, 65, 148, 187
Cilicia, Greeks of, 89
Claudius, Matthias, 132
Clausnitzer, Tobias, 129
Clement of Alexandria, 74, 93
Coleridge, Samuel T., 120
Collegia Pietatis, 129
Columbus, Christopher, 77
Compline, 77
Communion Service, 76-77
Confessions, of St. Augustine, 131
Constantine, Emperor, 188
Constantinople, 69, 92
Constantius, Emperor, 99
Cooke, Bishop, 76
Corpus Christi, 116
Council of Nicaea, 175, 188
Council of Toulouse, 63
Council of Trent, 115-16, 119
Coverdale, Miles, 63, 68, 74, 120, 136, 138
Courtship of Miles Standish, 156
Cox, Frances E., 150
Cultural immigration, 40, 42
Cuneiform writings, 55
"Cursing-Veda," 49

Damasus, Bishop, 113
Davies, Sir H. Walfred, 79
Davies, Samuel, 160
Dearmer, Canon Percy, 83, 108, 111, 129, 152
Deborah, 61
De contemptu mundi, 109
DePauw University, 16
De Profundis, 68
Dexter, Henry Martin, 93
Dickinson, Clarence, 31
Disciples, Church of the, 65
Dix, W. Chatterton, 151
Drese, Adam, 131
Duffield, Samuel W., 110
Duchesne, Père, 91
Dykes, John Bacchus, 109, 152, 185

Early Christian music, 72-74
Easter, 106, 116, 118
"Eastern Breviary," 94
Eastern Church, 62, 74, 85, 89, 94
Eaton, Edward Dwight, 183
Ecumenical Trends in Hymnody, 175, 183
Edward VI, 63, 136, 145
Egyptian hymns, 43, 56
Egyptian literature, 43-44
Egyptian Religions, 46
Elixer, The, 142-43
Elizabeth, Queen, 145
Ellerton, Canon John, 24, 151
Embury, Philip, 160
Enchiridion, 11
England, 62, 144
    18th century, 145
English Church (*see also* Church of England), 63, 65, 138, 142, 147, 149
English sacred poetry, 180
Enlightenment, era of, 132
Epaphroditus, 11
Ephraem, 91
Epictetus, 11, 19
Epistle, 112
Epworth, 145
Erman, Adolf, 44, 46, 48
Essenes, 73
Established Church (England), 146
Ethical Teachings in the Latin Hymns of Medieval England, 111
Eucharist, 133
Euphrates, 55
Evangelical (Lutheran) Church, 123, 129
Evangelical hymns, 149
Evangelicals, 129

Faber, Frederick W., 150
Farel, Guillaume, 132, 134
Federal Council of Churches, 175-76
Fellowship Hymn Book, 153
Ferial (chanting), 66
Fest-Ouvertüre, 126

Findlater, Sarah, 150
Fitzgerald, Edward, 70
"Folding" terms, 131
Foote, Henry Wilder, 187
Fortunatus, Venantius, 105-6
Foster, Stephen, 166
France, 62, 134
Frere, W. H., 127
Furneaux, Dean, 130

Gatty, Nicholas, 152
General Selection of the Newest . . . Hymns, A, 30
Geneva, 132, 136-37
Gerhardt, Paul, 108, 127-29
German chorale (-s), 122-25
Gillman, F. J., 153, 188-89
Gloria in Excelsis Deo, 66, 68, 72, 75-77, 89
Gloria Patri, 68, 78, 112, 117
Glorioso salvatoris, 111
Gnostic (-s), 91
Gnosticism, 90
Gogatsky, Carl H. von, 128
Golden Legend, 86
"Golden Sequence," 116
Good Friday, 116
Good Shepherd, 73
Goostly Psalms and Spritualle Songes, 74, 136, 138
Gordon, George A., 34, 155
Gospel, 112
Gospel Order Revised, The, 158
  books, 169
Gospel song (hymn), 168-70, 186
Gradual, 112, 126
Great Awakening, 62, 159
"Great Bible," 63, 69-70
"Greater Doxology," 76
"Great Entrance," 99
Greece, ancient, 59
Greek (-s), 73, 82, 89, 94, 96, 99
  culture, 73, 89
  drama, 73
  musical system, 74
  poetry, 94

Greek canon, 94
Greek Church, 94
Gregorian (service books), 118
Gregory, Arthur E., 23, 77
Gregory of Nazianzus, 94
Gregory the Great, 101 178
Griffith, Ralph T. H., 48
Grimm, 101
Gwyn, Nell, 142

Hagiolatry, 121
Handel, George F., 89
Hannah, 61
Harmon, Nolan B., 76
Harmonius, 91
Harrington, Karl P., 185
Hartford Selection, The, 162
Harvard, 187-88
Hastings, Thomas, 170
Haydn, F. J., 132
Haydn, J. M., 132
Heber, Reginald, 148
Hebrew poets and poetry, 42, 48, 56, 58
Hebrew poets and poetry, 42, 48, 56, 72
Hedge, Frederick H., 171
Henry VIII, 136, 138
Heptaméron, 136
Herbert, George, 28, 101, 138-39, 142, 154
Hermes, 73
Herod, 74
Herrnhut, 130
Hindu, 49-50
  mind, 49
  people, 48-50
  writers, 49
Hislop, D. H., 123
History of the Christian Church, 60
History of the Ritual, 76
Hodgin, E. Stanton, 133
Holmes, John Haynes, 34, 171
Holmes, Oliver Wendell, 171
Holmes, Thomas J., 159
Holst, Gustav von, 152

Homer, 89
Homeric hymns, 59
Horder, Garrett, 26
Hosanna, 79
Hosmer, Frederick Lucian, 171
"Hugenot Marseillaise," 157
Huneker, James Gibbon, 14
Hunter, Stanley A., 188
Huntington, William R., 81
Huss, John, 133
Hussites, 121
Hymn-Book of the Modern Church, The, 23
Hymn Society, 90
Hymn Tunes and Their Story, 179
Hymnals
  English, 152-53
  Evangelical and Reformed for Youth, 33
  Inter-Church, 182-83
  Lutheran, 183
  Oxford, 153
  Presbyterian, 65
Hymnary, The, (Canadian), 64
Hymnary, Menonnite, 177
Hymns Ancient and Modern, 150-51, 154
Hymns and Sacred Poems, 128,131
Hymns and Spiritual Songs (Baptist), 160; (Browne), 139; (Watts), 144
Hymns for Children, 167
Hymns for Those That Seek . . . Salvation, 84
Hymns of the Eastern Church, 95, 98
Hymns of the Kingdom, 153
Hymnus Angelicus, 89
Hymnus Optimus, 81

Iconoclastic controversy, 98
Ikhnaton Hymn to Aton, 43, 46
India, early history, 50
Indian poets, 50
Indo-Iranian, 49
Indra, 54

Instructor, The, 93
Intonation (chanting), 66
Introit, 117
Isadore of Seville, 101
Isaiah, 78
Isis, 45

Jacapone da Todi, 117
Jackson in F, 83
James II, 142
James, William, 27
Jeffries, Judge, 142
Jerome, 81, 113
Johnson, Samuel (Am.), 170
Johnson, Samuel (Eng.), 33
Jones, Edward Caldwell, 189
"Joyful Rhythm of St. Bernard," 107-8
Jubilee of 1739, 125
Jubilus, 113
Jubilate Deo, 68-70
Julian, John, 116, 146
Jumièges, Abbey of, 113-14

Kaisermarsch, 126
Kâlidâsa, 50
Kastalsky, 67
Keble, John, 33-34, 86, 150
Kellogg, George Dwight, 89
Ken, Bishop, 142
Kerr Lectures, 123
Kethe, William, 70, 137
Kirleison, 120
Knecht, Justin H., 132
Knights Templars, 69
Knox, John, 133, 137
Kyrie eleison, 79, 99, 117-18, 120

Lamentations, Assyrian, 58
Latest hymnals, 171
Lathbury, Mary A., 32
Latin hymns, 39, 96, 149
Lauds, 94
Laufer, Calvin W., 173
Lauxman, R., 127
Leavitt, Joshua, 162
Leichen, 120

Leisen, 120
Les Huguenots, 126
"Lesser Doxology," 78
Lighting of the Lamps, 86
Lightwood, James T., 179
Litanies, Assyrian, 58-59
Liturgical hymn, 149
Liturgy, 119
  Genevan, 134
  Modern, 99
  of Jerusalem, 99
  of St. James, 75, 85, 99
  Western, 99
Longfellow, H. W., 86, 156
Longfellow, Samuel, 32, 90, 115, 171
Long Meter Doxology, 142
Lord's Prayer, 69, 80
Louis I, King, 107
Lowell, James Russell, 171
Luther, Martin, 90, 108, 120-21, 123,
  125, 133-36, 138
Lutheran hymns, 122, 178
Lutherans, 127
Lutkin, Peter C., 76, 185
Lyra Americana, 186, 188

Maat, Egyptian goddess, 47
Macaronic hymns, 121
McConnell, Francis J., 19
Macdonald, K. S. 54
MacDougall, Hamilton C., 123
Magnificat, 61, 72, 74, 81
Mandalas, 51
Margaret, Queen of Navarre, 136
Marian refugees, 138
Mariolatry, 106, 117
Marlatt, Earl, 115
Marot, Clément, 136
Mary, Queen, 136
Mason, John, 139
Mason, Lowell, 170
Mass for the Dead, 116
Mather, Increase, 158
Mead, Steth, 30
Medial cadence, 66
Mediation (chanting), 66

Melisma (-ta, -tic), 112-15
Melodia, 113
Mendelssohn, Felix, 125
Messenger, Ruth E., 90, 111
Messiah, The, 89, 124
Meters, 53
  Ambrosian, 101
  ballad, 146
  Charles Wesley's use of, 147
  classic Greek, 90
  common, 53-54, 146
  long, 53, 101, 146
  lyric, 53, 90
  "peculiar," 53, 147
  Prudentius' use of, 102
  Rig-Veda, 53
  short, 53-54, 146
Meyerbeer, Giacomo, 126
"Midnight Hymn," 142
Milan, 62, 92, 100-1
Milman, Henry Hart, 148
Milton, John, 138
Miracle plays, 118
Miriam, 61
"Miss Hathaway's Experience," 165
Moffatt, James, 39
Monsell, J. S. B., 151
Morgan, Frank A., 182
Monk, W. H., 152
Montesquieu, C., 145
Morality plays, 118
Moravians, 130
Morning canticles, 74
Moses, 61
Moultrie, Gerald, 99
Mother Eve, 165
Müller, Max, 50
My Education and Religion, 155
Mystery plays, 118, 121

Nanak, 50
Nativity hymns, 72, 74, 127
Neale, John Mason, 94-95, 97-98,
  106-7, 109, 148, 150
Meander, Joachim, 129
Nestorians, 76

Nettleton, Asahel, 162
New Babylonians, 55
New Hymnal of Praise (Eaton), 183
"New Side" synod, 160
New Version, 139-40, 158
Newman, Cardinal, 90, 150-51
Newton, John, 115
Niceta, Bishop, 82
Nicolai, Otto, 126
Notker Balbulus, 90, 113-15, 121
Nunc dimittis, 68, 72, 77, 81

Offertory Sentence, 66
Old Scottish chant, 76
"Old Side" synod, 160
Old Version, 139-40, 155, 157
Opening sentence, 99
Order of the Gospel, The, 158
Ordinal, 63
Orpheus, 73
Osiris, 45
  hymn to, 45
Oxford Movement, 148-50

Palestrina, 67
Palmer, Ray, 108
Palm Sunday, 107, 127, 148
  processional, 107
"Pamphlet Library on Worship," 175
Parker, Caroline B., 183-84
Parkinson, William, 161
Parry in D, 83
Pastoral prayers, 80
Pawson, John, 25
Peasants' War, 133
Pentecost, 116
"Penitential Psalms," Assyrian, 58
Peri Stephanon, 103
Perowne, Bishop, 62, 71
Phillips, C. S., 126
Philo, 73
Philosopher's stone, 142
Pietist movement, 127, 129
Pietists, 129-31
Plain Acount of Christian Perfection, 128
Pliny, 73

Pocket Hymn Book, 162
Poets
  Indian, 50
  New England, 183, 187
  Quaker, 183
  Unitarian, 183
"Pointing," of chants, 65
Pott, Francis, 151
Pratt, Waldo Selden, 156, 169
Prayer Book (see *Book of Common Prayer*)
Pre-Watts era, 141
Price, Carl, 178
Primitive Christianity, 88
Primitive music, 41
Priscilla, 156
Procter, Adelaide A., 32
Prose (-s), medieval, 51, 79, 112, 114-15, 118
Prostrations, Assyrian, 58
Prudentius, 102-3, 106
Psalms of degrees, 112
Psalmus responsorius, 112
Psalters
  Ainsworth's, 156
  Anglo-Genevan, 137, 139
  English, 137, 139
  French, 139
  Genevan, 137
  John Daye's, 137
  New Version, 139-40, 158
  Old Version, 139-40, 155, 157
  Scottish, 139-40, 158
  Strassburg, 136
Puritan (-s), 69

Quaker, 183

Ra, hymn to (see Re)
Radegunda, Queen, 106
Re, hymn to, 44
Reed, Luther D., 183
Reeves, George, 176
Reformation
  German, 126
  Lutheran, 62, 100, 120
Reformation Festival, 125

Reformation Symphony, 126
Reformed (non-Lutheran) Church, 123, 133
Requiem Mass, 116
Responsorium graduale, 112
Revelation, Book of, 78
Rider, George T., 186-88
Rig-Veda, 48, 51-53
Riley, Athelstan, 152
Rinkart, Martin, 126
Robbins, Howard Chandler, 175, 178, 181
Robinson in F, 68
Robinson, John, 68
Romans, 60
Rood-cross, 112
Rood loft, 112
Rous, Francis, 140-41
Russian composers, 85

Sabbath School Bell, The, 166
Sackville College, 95
Sacred Latin Poetry, 104
St. Ambrose, 62, 82, 92, 100-3, 115, 120
St. Anatolius, 96-97
St. Augustine, 22-23, 27, 36, 82, 92, 108, 122, 131, 177
St. Francis Xavier, 111
St. Hilary, 99
St. Jerome, 81, 113
St. Paul, 27, 36, 88, 122
St. Benedict, Rule of, 82
St. Gall, Monastery, 90, 113
St. James, Liturgy of, 75, 85, 99
St. Margaret's Sisterhood, 96
St. Paul's London, 68
Sama-Veda, 49, 51
Sanctus, 117
Sankey, Ira D., 169
Sanskrit, 48-51
Savonarola, 133
Schaff, Philip, 26, 60, 107, 122, 179
Schütz, J. J., 129
Schmolck, Benjamin, 129-30
Selection of Hymns (Parkinson), 161

Sequence, medieval, 51, 79, 112-18, 121
Sequentia, 113
Sequentia cum prosa, 115
Service
  Anglican, 69-70
  Evening, 69-70
  in church usage, 68
  John Wesley, 70
  Morning, 69-70
  Sunday, 69
  Synagogue, 70, 73
"Seven Greater Antiphons," 111
Shakespeare, William, 138
Shaw, Bernard, 74
Shaw, Martin, 153
Shepherd, Thomas, 13 9
Sikh religion, 50
Simeon, 72, 77-78
Simpson, Bishop, 173
Singing schools, 168, 170
"Song of the Angels," 75
Song of the Hebrew Children, 79
Songs of Praise, 153
"Song of Songs," 74
Sophronius, 85
  Hymn to, 86
Spalatin, George, 121
Spectator, The, 144
Spener, P. J., 129
Spenser, Edmund, 138
Spitta, Carl J. P., 132
Stainer, Sir John, 81, 86, 152
Star of the East, 33
State Church, English, 63
Stead, William T., 84
Steele, Anne, 148, 184
Sternhold and Hopkins, 139, 155-56
Sternhold, Thomas, 136
Stone, Samuel J., 151
Strawbridge, Robert, 160
Strong, Nathan, 162
Sullivan, Sir Arthur, 152, 185
Sumerian (-s), 55, 57-58
  god, 57

hymns, 39
Sunday-school books, 166, 168
Sunday Service for America, 162
Sun Hymn, 46-47
Sursum Corda, 184
Switzerland, 62, 133-34
Synesius, 94
Synagogue, 60, 62, 70, 73
Syriac, 92
Syrian Christians, 91
Tammuz, 45
Tate and Brady, 139, 158-59
Tarsus, 89
Te Deum, 68, 79, 81-84
  German, 126
Telford, John, 74
Temple, The, 143
Temple worship, 61-62
Tennyson, Alfred, Lord, 34
Terminal cadence, 66
Termination (in chanting), 66
Tersanctus, 78, 89
Tersteegen, Gerhard, 131-32
Tertullian, 99
Theodulph of Orleans, 107
Therapeutate, 73
Thirty-nine Articles, 63
Thirty Years' War, 126-27, 129
"Thousand and One Hymns," 51
Three Centuries of American Hymnody, 187
Tillett, Wilbur F., 35
Tisserand, Jean, 118
Tractarian Group, 90
  Movement, 150
Trench, Archbishop, 102, 104, 108, 117
Trinity College, 187
Trope(-s, -ers), 112, 115, 117-18
Troubadours, 106
Tunes
  hymn, 117, 130, 152-53, 156
  "common," 146
  naming of, 184
  "Old Methodist," 147, 179
  "proper," 146

Tunes, names of
  Adeste Fideles, 184
  Ar-Hyd-y-Nos, 183
  Aughton, 184
  Austrian Hymn, 132
  Boylston, 184
  Dennis, 184
  Eucharist, 184
  Finlandia, 150, 183
  Foundation, 183
  Geibel, 184
  He Leadeth Me, 184
  Hamburg, 184
  Hanover, 184
  Innsbruck, 121
  Liebster Jesu, wir sind hier, 129
  Lobe der Herren, 129
  Lyons, 132, 184
  Martyrdom, 140
  Old 100th, 70, 126, 137, 140, 157-58
  Old 113th, 140, 157
  Old 134th, 140
  Portuguese Hymn, 184
  St. Agnes, 109
  St. Hilda, 132
  St. Michael, 140
  Ton-y-Botel, 183
  Toulon, 157
  Webb, 184
Tutor, The, 93
Tweedy, Henry Hallam, 115, 185
Tyndale, William, 63

Unitarians, 90, 159, 170, 183
Unitas Fratrum, 130
United Church of Canada, 64
United Brethren, 130
Upanishads, 51

Vaughan Williams, Ralph, 152
Veda (-s), 39, 48, 50-51, 54-56
Vedic ceremonies, 51
Vedic thought, 51
Vedic poets, 52
Venite, 67-69
Vespers, 74, 111

Village Hymns, 162
Virgin Mary, 106, 121

Wagner, Richards, 126
Walpole, Robert, 145
Walther, John, 136
Walton, Izaak, 142
Waters, Horace, 166
Watts, Isaac, 24, 33, 35, 37, 54, 90,
    102, 115, 139, 142-44, 148, 154,
    158-59, 161, 166, 178, 184, 187
Weissell, George, 127
Wesleyan Hymn Book, 165
Wesleyan Revival, 62, 147, 179
Wesley, Charles, 21-22, 35, 84, 102,
    115-16, 131, 146-48, 154, 165-
    67, 178, 187
    John, 12, 15, 22, 68-70, 128, 130-
    31, 140, 142, 145, 147, 150, 157,
    162, 184
    John and Charles, 90, 127-28, 131,
    144-45, 147
    Susannah, 142

Western Church, 62, 69, 74, 76, 82,
    86, 89, 92, 94, 100-1, 120
Western Record, 163
Whitefield, George, 159, 162
Whittier College, 176
Whittier, John Greenleaf, 49
"Wicked Polly" hymn, 163
Wilson, H. H., 53
Winkworth, Catherine, 127, 129, 150
Wiseman, F. Luke, 21
Wither, George, 141-42
Wittenberg, 62
Woodbury, I. B., 170
Wordsworth, Christopher, 151
Worship, defined, 12
Worship in Song (Parker), 183
Wycliffe, John, 133

Yajur-Veda, 49-51
Yale, 187
Young people, hymns for, 189

Zacharias, 72, 75, 78, 81
Zinzendorf, Count, 130-31
Zwingli, Huldreich, 133-34